In poignant flashes ɑ
Glenn walks us thɩ
with his mother during her decline with dementia. Grab
a copy of *Coffee with Mom* and be reminded of one
critically important message: Time is a very great gift,
especially in a season of goodbye.

Karen Kingsbury, #1 *New York Times*
bestselling author

There are 5.8 million Americans living with Alzheimer's
disease, which has also been described as a family disease, because it affects so many people surrounding
the patient. Pastor Mike Glenn gives us a window into
the details of his mother's battle with this illness, and
the ways he learned to cope and love her through it all.
Coffee with Mom helps us not feel so alone in our own
journeys. Alzheimer's is the only killer in the top ten in
this country with no treatment or cure, and I'm grateful to Mike for helping to raise awareness through his
personal, vulnerable, and honest story.

Kimberly Williams-Paisley, actress, author

Some days my ninety-year-old mother calls me and
tells me how my ninety-year-old father, her husband of
more than six decades, is doing. Sometimes I want to
say, "Mercy, mom, he's ninety," and sometimes I do,
but most times I just listen because there's not much to
say. Or do. But listen. There is no promise that we will
age gracefully or that the aged will be gracious in their
old age. Sometimes we and they do, but not very often
if what I hear from others is accurate. Aging is hard but
I'm not sure it is as hard as caring for the aging. Most
of the time you aren't sure you are caring well, even
when your caring comes straight from a heart of love
for your aging mom or dad. Mike Glenn's story of his
mom is a story of a woman gradually dying, of a son

gradually grieving, of a life gradually ending, and of a pastor gradually letting go of an unforgettable life of an unforgettable mom. He learned what kind of son he was—a mighty fine one, if you ask me. This is a love story, a son for a mother. Mike, my friend, had to learn that he was okay with his caring for his mom. He was better than okay."

Dr. Scot McKnight, author, speaker, professor

Mike Glenn and I walked a similar journey and, in the end, had the distinct honor of caring for and serving the first person that cared for and served each of us. In my case—it was my dad who struggled with dementia in his latter years. In Mike's case, it was his mom who was diagnosed with Alzheimer's. In both cases, it became one of the most difficult and one of the most honoring opportunities of our lives. Mike and I have been friends for years. We have so many of the same interests and concerns. We both are crusaders for justice, for racial unity, and so many other things. But I believe our strongest connecting point was each of our callings to being a caregiver to a parent patient. Whether you find yourself in a similar situation or whether you know someone who is—this is a fabulous love story of a son loving and caring for his mother.

Michael W. Smith, singer, songwriter

Mike Glenn's sharing of his mom's wit, wisdom, and the heart break of Alzheimer's is a treasure. I followed their story personally as his friend and through the tweets of her thoughts of the day. I laughed, cried, and was proud of both of them on their final journey together. You will be too.

Dave Ramsey, #1 bestselling author

Coffee with Mom

MIKE GLENN

Coffee with Mom

Caring for a parent with dementia

B&H
PUBLISHING
NASHVILLE, TENNESSEE

978-1-5359-4901-9

Published by B&H Publishing Group
Nashville, Tennessee

Dewey Decimal Classification: 616.8
Subject Heading: ALZHEIMER'S DISEASE /
BRAIN—DISEASES / DEMENTIA

Cover illustration © Taaron Parsons.

1 2 3 4 5 6 • 23 22 21 20 19

*This book is dedicated to my mom,
Barbara Bustin Glenn, who taught me to
do the very things that aggravated her so.*

*And to my brothers and sisters, known
and unknown, who are on this journey
with someone they love.*

Contents

Introduction

I didn't start out to write a book. Like most people who are dealing with family members who have Alzheimer's or dementia, I was just trying to survive. My mom had been diagnosed with Alzheimer's and dementia in the fall of 2014. I had moved her to Morning Pointe Assisted Living and Memory Care in the winter of that year.

Both Jeannie, my wife, and I were working in demanding jobs. She was a triage phone nurse for the Vanderbilt Hospital Clinics in Williamson County, and I was the pastor of Brentwood Baptist Church. Our boys were married and well into their careers, and Jeannie and I were new grandparents. Our lives were full and good.

Then, we added Mom.

My family situation meant I would become Mom's primary and sole caregiver. We chose Morning Pointe in Brentwood because it was very close to our house. We could be there in minutes. It was also on my way to the church. I could stop by and have coffee with her on my way into my office.

That's what I did. For four years, not every morning, but several times a week, I would stop and have coffee with Mom while she ate her breakfast. Sometimes she'd be in a good mood, and we'd laugh as we told old family stories. Other days, she'd be angry, and I'd be accused, attacked, and condemned, and yes, some days, cussed out. Still other days, she'd be sad and unable to find a reason to live.

In our conversations, she would say things, and I'd write them down. Some of them were funny, some were angry, and others were just the stuff of life. They were all honest, and they were all her. Friends would accuse me of making up her quotes, but I didn't. I would edit them to fit into the limitations of Twitter, but other than that, everything in *Coffee with Mom* is 100 percent her.

When I started publishing her quotes, people started coming up to me and telling me their own stories. "My mom said that," they would say. Or, "I went through that with my dad." Or simply, "I'm praying for you." I soon discovered I was in a very large family of people who were related by having a loved one with Alzheimer's or dementia. They didn't talk about it a lot because they knew no one would understand. Unless you've been there, you don't know what it does to your soul to see the woman who taught you about integrity and honesty start stealing everything that wasn't nailed down. When you asked her about it, she'd tell you her mother gave it to her and fight you if you tried to take it away.

Caring for an Alzheimer's patient means you hurt all the time. "Coffee with Mom" was one of the ways I dealt with my own grief. I was surprised to find out it had helped a few others as well.

In the following pages, I share some of our stories. This isn't a comprehensive history of the last four years of Mom's life nor is it any kind of medical account. This is one son's story of trying to love his mom the best way he knew how.

First, you need to hear something I wrote for you called "Put On Your Oxygen Mask." Chances are you are here because you don't know if you can do this. Breathe. With the Lord's help, you can. Second, I want you to meet Mom. This is one way our stories are not the same—there's no one else like my mom. And you can probably say the same about yours. To know my mom, you've got to know about John, so I will introduce you to my dad too. The remainder of the book, I hope, will narrate our stories in a way that will share some things we learned along the journey. Some things we did well. Others we could have done better. But my hope is that you find your story inside of, or adjacent to, my story. I hope you'll see that you are not alone.

Throughout the book, you will find quotes I published online between 2014 and 2018 that came from our time together over coffee. They are labeled "Coffee with Mom." Some are funny. Others are laugh-to-keep-from-crying funny. All of them were my mom.

Mom died in July while I was writing this book. The hardest part of my writing has been to go back and change the verbs from present tense to past tense.

So, I dedicate this book to all of those caregivers who are trying to love someone with this disease. Too many days, there are no right or wrong answers. There's only "this is the best I can do." This is the question that haunts us: "Am I doing everything I can do?" The short answer is we can't do everything we want to do, but we're probably doing all we need to do. If you're showing up and loving them well, you're doing the best you can do.

And in the end, we will be okay with that.

It will be enough.

Chapter 1

Put On Your Oxygen Mask

The nursing supervisor slid her stethoscope carefully over my mom's chest. She stopped, turned her head slightly, and focused her listening. She stood up and looked at me. "I'm sorry, Mr. Glenn, but I'm not getting anything. Your mother is gone."

I was sitting in a chair next to my mom's bed, stroking her forehead and hair, waiting for the nurse to tell me what I already knew. Mom was gone. I'd been losing her a little bit at a time for four years, and now, in the stillness of Williamson Medical Center on this Saturday afternoon, it was over.

> **Coffee with Mom:**
> Grief catches me at the strangest times. I can hear a song, recognize a smell, or see an old photograph, and instantly I become a nine-year-old boy who misses his mom.

Mom was gone.

And I cried and cried like a little boy. I cried and cried like it was the first time I had heard the news. I wasn't ready for this. You'd think I would be, but I wasn't ready for this. Whenever you lose your mother, you're nine years old inside. I became an orphan in that moment.

I know that sounds funny. After all, I was sixty-one years old, and my mom was eighty-one, but that's exactly how I felt. I was all alone in the world. I was an orphan.

Early in my ministry, I led a funeral service for the ninety-five-year-old matriarch of a family. As we left the graveside and started walking toward our cars, Charlie, her youngest son, fell apart. He began crying, his shoulders heaving as he tried to push off the weight of his grief.

"I'm an orphan," he told me. "I'm an orphan, Mike."

"Charlie," I said, "you're sixty-five years old. You're too old to be an orphan."

"No, I'm not," he insisted. "I'm nobody's little boy anymore."

All of these years later, sitting in my mom's hospital room, I remembered my conversation with Charlie. He was right. When your second parent dies, you're an orphan. It doesn't matter how old you are or how old your parent is, when they die, you feel a loneliness in the world you really can't explain. You're nobody's little . boy anymore.

I was an orphan.

I was surprised by the depth of my grief. I had been grieving for four years. I thought I had cried all of the tears I had to cry. I really thought when my mom did die, I wouldn't cry that much. In fact, I had actually worried about it. What if people thought I didn't love my mom because I didn't cry all that much? I needn't have worried.

With a disease like Alzheimer's, you lose your loved one by degrees. I had been losing Mom little bit by little bit over the last four years. Every time she lost an ability, every time I had to take something away, or she forgot a story, I would grieve. Your grief is like a dull toothache that never goes away. You hurt all of the time. Your pain is never enough to shut you down, but it does rob your days of joy.

Anytime I was by myself, anytime my thoughts would wander off, I would go back to the latest confrontation with my mother and rethink everything. Could I have said something differently? Could I have done something differently? Was there something else I needed to do? I never could find a satisfactory answer. I was always second-guessing myself. That only added to the anxiety of the grief. I would go over and over every situation and every moment again and again.

When I first noticed something was wrong with Mom, I cried. I cried all of the way from Huntsville to Nashville. I did that a lot.

I cried because my mom was scared. Whenever I was visiting her and told her I had to go back to Nashville, she would beg me to stay. "Just spend the night and go home in the morning," she would say. I would tell her I couldn't, that I had some early morning meetings. Most of the time that was true, but sometimes it wasn't.

Sometimes, I just couldn't stay. I had to leave. I couldn't stay in Huntsville, where the absence of my dad created a hole so large it allowed all of the air in the atmosphere to escape. I couldn't breathe. The weight was too heavy, and some days I could barely walk. I knew the day was coming when I would have to take over, but on these days, I just couldn't do it.

I know I should have been stronger. I know I should have been bolder and more confident, but here's what I couldn't understand or get anyone else to understand. Yes, I knew something was wrong with Mom. She had lost my dad. She was grieving. She was lonely. She was hurting. She was afraid about the future.

But I was grieving too.

Anytime I went to my mom's and dad's home in Huntsville, I kept looking for Dad to be there. Whenever I would walk into the house, the first thing that would hit me was my dad wasn't there. I had to deal with my own grief. My dad was bigger than life, and his absence left a huge hole in our world.

But I never had time to cry for my dad. Mom quickly needed my full attention. From the haze of trying to grieve my dad's death, I was having to try to discern subtle, but real, changes in my mom's life. Where was Dad's insurance information? Mom didn't know.

"Mom, we need to go change the property to your name. Do you have any paperwork?" Yes, she did, somewhere. We just never found that "somewhere." Everything we did had to be done from scratch. I had to explain to every vendor, renter, government official, and banker that I was having to get my mom's affairs in order, and I was trying to close out Dad's business affairs after his death. I was a little overwhelmed.

Thankfully, nearly everyone knew my parents, and was eager to help. They would pull out the needed forms and show me where to sign. Eventually, we got everything squared away, but it was needlessly difficult and tedious. Mom couldn't find anything, but we had to look. We spent hours going through filing cabinets and stacks of paper. She kept forgetting her passwords. Every time we tried to set up something so she wouldn't have to worry about it, she'd forget the password, or forget where we put it . . . and worry about it anyway.

Today she'd know a story, and tomorrow she wouldn't. Today she would know everyone in the picture, but tomorrow she wouldn't. She didn't remember her birthday. She didn't remember mine. It's a cold day when your mother doesn't remember your birthday. Sure, you know it's the illness, but it doesn't help. She didn't know my birthday, and I wondered would the day come when she didn't know me.

And you grieve again.

Here's the reality. You can't grieve all of the time. You can't hold up under the constant, squeezing pressure. One of the growing concerns of the healthcare community is the health of the caregiver. If you're the primary caregiver, especially if the patient is being kept at home, you can quickly ruin your own health. Lack of sleep, verbal abuse, and sometimes physical abuse can take a heavy toll on your life. You have to learn to take care of yourself and not feel guilty about it. No one is helped if the caregiver goes down.

At first, this is hard to deal with. For one thing, you created this problem, right? You're the one who made her unhappy, and if so, then you have to be responsible for making her happy again, right?

> **Coffee with Mom:** If you're the primary caregiver, don't forget to take care of yourself. That means rest, proper nutrition, and exercise . . . and time with God. It doesn't help anyone if you break down too.

Wrong. You didn't do anything to cause these problems. The illness did. You got it just like your patient did, which means you have to undergo treatment just like they are. Now, that may not mean taking medication or frequent doctors' visits, but it does mean submitting to a disciplined regiment to make sure you're in good enough health to take care of your loved one.

First, don't be afraid to ask for help. I know a lot of people who have suffered from the guilt of having to put their husband or wife in a facility when they were no longer able to take care of them at home. By the time a situation has come to this, more times than not, we're past the time when a decision should have been made. For your safety and for their safety, you have to make the hard call.

You can't watch them twenty-four hours a day, and if you don't, they walk off or drive off. They open drawers and doors and get into things that can be harmful to them. It's the old, "I took my eye off of them for one moment . . ." and somebody gets hurt. That's a lot harder to live with than placing them in a facility.

We learned to keep journals. We found out that while we may not feel like sitting down at the end of the day and writing everything down, we couldn't rely on our memories. Things happen too fast to keep it all mentally catalogued. Too many things happen for you to remember every detail. When they happen, you don't think you'll ever forget this moment, but you do.

I used to use the plural "we" when I talked about Mom having Alzheimer's. "She" didn't have Alzheimer's, "we" did. I found myself unable to remember anything from one moment to the next, and then, when I got to the doctor, I couldn't remember Mom's symptoms or how the medicine had helped. Too many times, I just ended up telling the doctor everything was fine. I was just too overwhelmed to remember anything.

The changes are too subtle, too numerous, and happen too quickly. One day you'll notice one thing. The next day you'll notice something else. In between those days, ten other things will happen. How will you keep it all straight? How will you notice the patterns? The only way you'll be able to do this is to keep a journal.

Not only will you need to have a place to write down the details of your loved one's care, but you'll need a space to write down what you're going through emotionally. There will be days when you get so angry you will think you'll explode. My mom would say some outrageous things to me. She would accuse me of crimes and misdemeanors. More than once, she told me she was going to report me to the police and have me arrested for elder abuse, burglary, robbery, and fraud. She told me that giving me her power of attorney was the worst mistake she ever made.

What do you do with all of this emotion? You write it down. If you don't write it down, the anger, grief, and frustration just circle around in your head and your heart. You won't be able to think about anything else. If you write it down, you'll give your emotions somewhere to go. You'll be able to recognize patterns, and yes, you'll be able to recognize the ridiculousness of some of the things that have been said.

And you'll be able to remember some good things as well. Inevitably, when I would start writing about my conversations with my mom, I would remember another time and another place. I would find myself smiling.

There were things I had forgotten, and other things I hadn't thought about in a long time. I wrote them down as well. I got back a lot of family stories doing this. Reminding myself of who my mom used to be gave me a little more reason to take care of her one more day.

And yes, you'll need to take some breaks, but be warned, don't go too far if you do. One time Jeannie and I took a Mediterranean cruise. I got to see all of the historical places, statues, and works of art I had always read about and studied. During the cruise, we got an emergency phone call saying my mom had been taken to the emergency room. By the time we had run everything down and found out what was going on, Mom had woken up that morning telling everyone she was deaf in her right ear.

She had always been deaf in her right ear.

The acoustic neuroma had taken her hearing four years before. For whatever reason, she had gotten up that morning and forgotten she was deaf, so her not being able to hear was a totally new experience for her. Trying to handle all of that through international long distance was a nightmare.

Here's the thing you have to remember: this is a marathon, not a sprint. This is a long journey of countless days, cloudy skies, and sometimes thick fog that makes it impossible to get anywhere. But today, you do what you have to do. Tomorrow, you'll do what has to be done on that day.

And every day, you'll remember your pain. It never goes away. This is the price of love. You can't do anything to make it go away, but you can keep it from swamping your little boat. If you go under, so does your loved one. You have to learn to keep your head above water.

> **Coffee with Mom:** What feels like exhaustion is actually grief. There's a weariness to grief that drains you of all of your emotional, physical, and mental energy. Be sure you handle it before it handles you.

When you get on an airplane, the flight attendant will inform you about how the oxygen masks will deploy in case of an emergency. They will then tell you that if you're traveling with someone, put your oxygen mask on first, then put the mask on your loved one. If you don't, you'll both pass out.

Your loved one is counting on you just like my mom counted on me. Put on your oxygen mask first.

Chapter 2

Meet My Mom

When I was growing up, I thought my mom was normal. Every child does. You don't remember the day you met your mom. You just opened your eyes one day and there she was. Every other day you opened your eyes, she was there, and so you grow up assuming that every child had a mother like yours.

> **Coffee with Mom:**
> (after I reminded her
> I was taller than her)
> "Makes no matter.
> You'll sit down for
> me to slap you."

It took me a few years, but I began to understand my friends didn't have a mother like mine. No one had a mother like mine.

There were enough clues in my early life for me to pick up that I was the son of a very unique mother. For one thing, she never let me win at anything. If we were playing checkers, Mom wouldn't let you win. If we were playing "Go Fish," she wouldn't let you win. If we were playing basketball in the driveway, Mom wouldn't let you win. She lettered in high school basketball, and she was known to slam you if you were driving toward the rim. "When you beat me," she said, "it'll mean something."

To understand my mother, you'd first have to know my mother had no adolescence. She was never a teenager. Whatever experiences and changes you go through between childhood and adulthood, my mother never made. The event that defined my mom's life happened when she was twelve years old. Her mother died of breast cancer. When she was diagnosed, my grandmother was sent to Jackson, Mississippi, for treatment. At the time, cobalt radiation was usual protocol. Years later, my mother could still describe in vivid detail how the radiation treatments burned her mother.

And she would also describe in great detail how her father looked when he came through the door that night to tell my mother and her three sisters that their mother had died.

My grandmother was a musician, and she was the one who had taught my mother to sing and play the piano. My grandmother had insisted my mother take piano lessons. Music was something my grandmother and mother shared. My mom would tell me about listening to her mother play the piano when she was growing up. Funny, but I grew up the same way—listening to my mother play the old hymns and gospel songs on the piano. I'm not sure I ever fully appreciated what my mom lost in the death of her mother.

I don't know what happened in that moment after her mother passed away. I don't know if someone said something. Something people usually say without thinking at a time like this, such as, "Well, Barbara, your sisters will be depending on you now." I don't know if my grandmother had said something to my mother about taking care of her sisters, but whatever it was, my mother instantaneously became an adult.

My mom became mother to her sisters overnight.

She dressed them for school. She took them to church. One of her friends told me she remembered the Bustin girls walking into church like four little ducks and sitting on the front row while Mom attended choir practice.

One afternoon, Mom thought the sisters had been particularly good during the week. She wanted to buy them a treat, so she piled them all in the car and drove them to the local ice cream parlor. When she got there and parked, the sheriff walked over to the car and asked to see her license. She told him she didn't have a license, and the funny thing is the sheriff knew she didn't have a license. He also knew what was going on in her family.

"Tell your father to get you a license," he told her.

"I can't. I'm not old enough."

"You were old enough to drive over here. You're old enough for a license."

That was my mom. She didn't give one thought about whether or not she should do or if she could do it. This was what needed to be done, and she was going to do it . . . even if it was against the law.

My grandfather worked at the Masonite plant in Laurel, Mississippi, and although they lived in the middle of extended family, Mom felt like she became responsible for her little sisters from that moment on. That dynamic made growing up among the Bustin girls interesting. My mom was their older sister and their mother, and her little sisters treated her that way well into their adulthood. All the resentments, dependencies, jealousies, anger, joys, secrets, love, and loyalty that happen between daughters and mothers, big sisters and little sisters, happened with my mom and her sisters all at the same time.

My grandfather remarried, and it wasn't a good situation, so my mom got a job at the local department store and moved into a small apartment. Even then, her sisters would come and stay at her apartment rather than being at home with their father. That was just the way life was. Mom took care of her sisters. Life isn't fair, my mom would later remind me, and once you understand how unfair life is, you'll be fine.

My grandfather's second marriage ended in divorce, and he married again. This marriage was a very stable one, and the sisters were able to experience a normal life. Yet, even with my grandfather's remarriage, the sisters always looked to Mom as their mother. When one of the sisters went through a painful divorce, she moved to Huntsville where my mother lived. She didn't move to Mississippi where the family was.

When one of the sisters got very sick, Mom flew out and took care of her. Okay, maybe I said that too nicely. My mom flew out and took over. Doctors and nurses were reporting in to my mom. Physical therapists were informing my mom about my aunt's progress, and if Mom wasn't satisfied, they redid the therapy. My aunt got better. She was too scared of my mom not to.

If I could only tell you one story about my mom, I would tell you this one. When my brother was sixteen years old, his best friend was killed in a car wreck. This was a devastating time for our family and community. I was at college, and by the time I got home, everyone had gathered at the funeral home. When I walked in, I'll never forget what I saw. My brother was standing by his friend's coffin and crying. My mother was standing there with him, crying too. That was my mom. Life was hard. Life wasn't fair. She knew that. But you were going to get through it, and she would stand right there with you until you did.

But Mom had another chapter in the adventure of her life and that was her marriage to my dad. They were married for more than fifty-seven years and grew so close they literally became one name: "JohnandBarbara." You never saw one without seeing the other. The great love story started one night when my mom and her friends went roller-skating. While they were skating, the girls—especially my mom—were being harassed by a lanky, skinny-legged skater who would circle them on one lap, and blow past them on the next lap. Eventually, he tripped my mom, and that's how my mom and dad met. When my mom would tell the story, she said she got up off of the rink floor and told her friends, "He'll pay for that. I'm going to marry him."

And she did.

> **Coffee with Mom:** "Your dad and I were married fifty-seven years. People say that's a long time, but it's not. It's not very long at all."

Don't Mess with John

My dad was twenty-three, and my mom had just turned nineteen when they got married. I was born when she was twenty. Mom and Dad were married so long and grew so close they literally became one person. I know you think I'm exaggerating, but I'm not. Where Mom was strong, Dad was weak. Where Mom was weak, Dad was strong. Dad was the visionary, and Mom took care of the details. Dad would do the sales at the store, and Mom would take care of the books. Dad would run for political office, and she would run his campaign. The challenges and struggles of their lives welded them together in such a way that not only

> **Coffee with Mom:**
> "Did Alabama win? Good. Your daddy was miserable to live with when they lost." (I know. I got that from him!)

couldn't they be pulled apart, but most of the time you couldn't tell where one stopped and the other started.

For most of their lives, they only had each other. Dad joined the Air Force to escape the poverty of south Mississippi. The Air Force trained my father on radars, and from Alexandria, Louisiana, to Gulfport, Mississippi, and finally Huntsville, Alabama, my mother followed my father out of Mississippi to the booming city of Huntsville, Alabama. My dad left the Air Force and became a civilian instructor for the Hawk missile at Redstone Arsenal. With both NASA and the Army missile command located in Huntsville, the city began to grow at a frenetic pace due to President Kennedy's desire to put a man on the moon and the Cold War with the Soviet Union. The rocket technology used for the space missions was then appropriated by the Department of Defense to bolster our nuclear arsenal at the height of the Cold War. Werner von Braun lived and worked in our town. People were being assigned to Huntsville from all over the country.

This made Huntsville a great town in which to grow up. Our teachers, mostly the spouses of NASA engineers and career military personnel, were highly educated, well-traveled, and interesting teachers. I had extraordinary teachers, and science was especially challenging and fun. We had rockets that blasted off in our science fairs, and the study of the universe in our classes was challenging because it was what our parents really did for a living.

Dad was an instructor of the radar system of the Hawk missile. Any nation using the Hawk system came to Huntsville to be trained, and my dad would be one of those who trained them. He was good at what he did and was commended for his excellence on numerous occasions. He would begin teaching at 7:30 in the morning, and he'd be done at 3:30 in the afternoon. That left half of a day for Dad to do something else.

His lack of a college education limited his ability to be promoted within the government services. So, Dad found other ways to provide for his family. He started repairing televisions in our garage. For most of my life, we never parked our cars in the garage—it was always filled with rows and rows of televisions my dad was repairing. People would bring over their televisions, and Dad would fix them. Most of the time when I went to bed, Dad would still be in the garage working on someone else's TV.

Mom and Dad were great partners. He was the creative visionary that came up with the ideas, and she was the nuts-and-bolts thinker that made things work. They built a very successful television and appliance business (Ray-Mar TV). Dad was the salesperson, and Mom was everything else. He was a successful community leader, and she was the one who made sure he made all of his meetings on time and rehearsed his speeches before he left. My dad was very self-conscious about his lack of education, so Mom would coach him about how to speak in public and how to make sure his verbs and nouns matched. Sometimes it helped. But most of the time, Dad was just himself. He couldn't help it. Mom would get so angry when he misspoke in public, especially if it was something she had coached him on. Dad was going to succeed. Mom would make sure of it.

Ray-Mar TV opened when I was in grade school and operated as a successful business until after I was married. Even then, Dad reluctantly sold the business when Mom told him she wasn't working anymore. Without his HR director, CFO, VP of Customer Relations, and Executive Assistant, my dad was forced to let the business go. As my father said at the time, "Son, your mama has made up her mind, and once she's made up her mind, there's no changing it."

She wouldn't change her mind, and she never apologized. She would just pick up and go on like nothing had happened. That was my mom. No excuses. No whining. No apologies and no self-pity. Life wasn't fair. Life wasn't easy. If the going got tough, bow your neck and get tougher. Find a way to get through. That was her answer to everything. Her philosophy was to grab the problem by the neck and shake it until an answer fell out.

Growing up, we learned to never complain to Mom. My dad would have sympathy for you, but Mom never would. If things weren't going your way, either let it alone or change it. Either way, make up your mind quickly and get to it. Just stop complaining. That was my mom.

For the most part, this philosophy of life served my mom well.

Mom became a fierce protector of my dad. My dad was a genuinely loving and trusting man. As a result, he was taken advantage of in business deals and political situations. Nothing would make my mother angrier than seeing someone take advantage of Dad.

One morning when Dad and I were at breakfast, he mentioned how Mom could never let anything go. Dad went on and said Mom should just forgive this person we were talking about. I told Dad that would never happen. He asked me why.

"Because," I said, "Mom only has one rule: 'Don't mess with John.' Break that rule and Mom will have nothing to do with you."

Dad looked at me as if he wanted me to explain what I had just said. I mentioned two people's names. The first was a political enemy who had betrayed Dad in a key moment of his political career. The second was a trusted ally and friend.

I named the first man. "Mom won't have anything to do with him," I said. "Why not?"

Dad said, "Because he lied to me."

"Exactly," I said. Then, I named the second man. "Now, he was known to drink a little bit and didn't go to church as much as Mom would have liked, but Mom loved him. Why?"

"Because he was my friend."

"Exactly. Mom isn't hard to understand. She only has one rule: 'Don't mess with John.'"

If anyone ever doubted that, their questions were answered when Dad had his heart attack. Early one morning at the end of 1988, my dad went to the doctor with a bad case of indigestion. As he described his symptoms, an alert nurse recognized my father was having a heart attack. He was ushered back into an examination room, and the doctor and his staff began to run a series of tests. Dad lost consciousness during the exam. He was rushed to the emergency room of Huntsville Hospital. His doctors and their teams worked for hours trying to stabilize him. When they finally did, it was determined my father would need major bypass surgery. He would end up having five bypasses. During the surgery, the doctor would send a member of his team out to talk to us. Dad was sicker than anyone had thought. The surgery was longer and more difficult than we had been told.

Mom found a new mission in life. She would take care of my dad. She would be his nurse, his counselor, his trainer, his nutritionist, and anything else he needed to make sure he lived as long and as well as he possibly could. They bought a lake house on the Tennessee River just outside of Scottsboro, and it became the center of our families' lives. Mom made sure of it. Mom decorated the house so whoever came was comfortable. She would cook whatever her grandchildren wanted to eat. Every holiday was centered at the lake house, with everyone gathered around Big John's (my dad) chair.

Mom watched Dad like a hawk. She monitored his salt intake, his calorie count, how much fat he had eaten, and the amount of sugar he had. She successfully removed all salt from his diet, to the point that my dad began to experience painful muscle cramps. When they tested his blood in the doctor's office, the doctor told Dad he had no salt in his system. Mom reminded the doctor he had said for Dad to cut out salt. So, she cut out salt—completely.

That's my mom. It's all or nothing.

Eventually, caring for my dad like this began to take a toll on my mom's health. She started suffering from headaches and acute vertigo. She brushed it off as the fatigue and stress of caring for my dad. As the symptoms worsened, she finally went to the doctor on her own. She was diagnosed with an acoustic neuroma, a benign tumor that grows on the balance nerve near where the hearing, balance, and facial nerves come together at the base of the brain. The result is usually deafness in the affected ear, loss of balance, and other symptoms as well.

A very invasive laser procedure was suggested to my mom. She would have had to endure several hours of surgery and several months of recovery. My mother never considered it. She wouldn't leave my dad that long.

As Dad's condition worsened, Mom did whatever she could do to keep my dad optimistic, hopeful, and eager to be alive. She willed him to stay alive. She watched his food, his exercise, and his social engagement. She would insist he stay engaged in his social life, buying him memberships in the Rotary Club and the Huntsville Quarterback Club. She made him get up and get dressed, and if need be, she'd put him in the car and would drive him around town to see their friends. Dad would often call me, and when I would ask him where he was, he would tell me he was walking behind "your mother in Walmart. You know your mother and Walmart."

Because I knew how committed Mom was to Dad, I dismissed it when he told me he was worried about Mom. "Something's wrong with your mama," he would say. When I would ask him to explain what he was worried about, he would tell me she had forgotten to pay the house payment on time, or didn't pay the utility bill, or she had forgotten something at one of the rental properties. And she would have forgotten, but in my mind, I was surprised she hadn't forgotten more. Caring for Dad was a twenty-four-hour, seven-days-a-week job. I don't know how she did it for as long as she did. If she forgot to pay a bill or two, that was to be expected. My mom was overloaded.

Dad did pretty well for a long time. He lived over twenty years after his first heart attack. I didn't realize how significant that was until I talked to my father's doctor at his funeral. According to the doctor, my dad was given five years after his first heart attack.

But you can only do so much. It was only a matter of time before my dad's heart finally gave out. As my dad's heart grew weaker, there were monthly trips to the hospital for stays of several days at a time. He broke his hip and had to have surgery. Of course, this meant an extended rehab. My mom was determined to exhaust every avenue she could. Dad was sent to a hospital in Nashville to see if he was a candidate for special treatment. Everything short of a heart transplant was considered. Finally, having exhausted every avenue of treatment, my dad was sent home to live out his time.

Mom cared for him around the clock. My mom ended up sleeping on the couch for two years because Dad was so restless at night. How she endured it, I'll never know. She was tired. She was overwhelmed. She was grieving the inevitable. And yes, she forgot some things. Any woman who was going through that would have a lot of grace from me if she forgot a few things.

Dad kept insisting, "Something's wrong with Barbara." I should have listened to him. If anyone knew her, it would have been him.

The phone rang a little after four in the morning. We had been expecting the call. My father was dying of congestive heart failure, and the doctors had told us we were running out of time. We thought we had a few days. We only had a few hours. My wife, Jeannie, and I were on the road in a few minutes and got to Huntsville way too quickly to have driven a safe speed. We got to be with my dad during his last few hours. We sang with Dad. We prayed with him. We told him how much we loved him, and how proud we were he was our dad.

At 2:30 in the afternoon, my dad passed away. "Lord, have mercy on me," he whispered, and he turned his head to the side and died. I don't want to be overly dramatic, but a part of my mom died with him.

In the aftermath of my father's death, I began to see what my father had been talking about.

My first clue about what I was beginning to deal with was when Daddy's headstone was delivered. We had ordered his headstone a few weeks before, and now it was being delivered. For the workmen to set the stone on the grave, you had to be there and pay off the balance owed on the work. If you weren't there or if you couldn't pay, they wouldn't take the headstone off the truck. Mom had called me and told me they were going to deliver the headstone the next morning.

I went down the next morning and took Mom out to breakfast. Then, we met the truck and the workers delivering the headstone. They handed me the bill, and I took it over to Mom. She got out her checkbook and wiped her hands over the page as if she was trying to straighten the pages. She put her hand over her mouth and started to cry.

"Mom, what's wrong?"

"I just miss your daddy so much. I just don't know what to do."

I didn't know if she meant she didn't know what to do in that moment, or if her grief had frozen her leaving her unable to do anything at all. Then, she looked at me, and I'll never forget the look in her eyes. She was lost. She didn't know what to do next. She was drowning.

I don't know if I can get you to understand this, but my mom never asked me for help—ever. Mom never admitted that things were beyond her control. There was never a situation when my mom didn't know what to do next. My mom ALWAYS knew what to do next.

But she didn't know this time. She was confused. She panicked. For a quick moment, she didn't know where she was or what she was supposed to do.

"Mom, let me take care of it and we'll figure it out later." So, I paid for the headstone, and we went home. She settled down, and we had a pretty good day.

Coffee with Mom:
"I didn't think you'd ever get here. Refill my coffee before you sit down like a good boy."

But I should have listened to Dad. Something was wrong with Mom. I thought it was just her grief, but it wasn't. Something was wrong, and it wasn't going to get better.

Chapter 4

Something's Wrong with Mom

The neurosurgeon walked into the examination room where Mom, Jeannie, and I were waiting. He flipped on the light box hanging on the wall to reveal an MRI of a human brain. It was Mom's brain. A normal brain scan looks like a halved melon with two dark kidney-shaped areas in the center; one side exactly like the other.

> Coffee with Mom:
> "Alzheimer's?
> Who said I have
> Alzheimer's?
> Whatever doctor told
> you that is an idiot."

My mom's MRI was scattered with white splotches.

"The neuroma isn't your mother's only problem," the doctor said.

"What do you mean?"

"See the scan," he said. "In a healthy brain, there should be two dark areas in the center of the scan. Your mom's brain scan is solid white. This isn't what we'd expect for someone of your mom's age."

"What does that mean?"

"I couldn't really tell you without more tests, but most of the time when we see scans like this, we're dealing with some type of vascular dementia. That means your mom's brain has been clogged by tiny little strokes from high blood pressure, diet, stress."

"Alzheimer's?"

"Probably some of both—Alzheimer's and vascular dementia."

My mom broke in, "Do I have Alzheimer's? Who said I have Alzheimer's?"

"No one, Mom. The doctor is saying we have to run more tests." I turned to the doctor, "What's vascular dementia?"

> "The easiest way to explain it to you is your mom has had hundreds of microscopic strokes throughout her brain. We can try medication to try and limit the progression of the disease, but most of the time, an illness like this is progressive despite treatment."

"What does that mean?"

"It means after we take care of the neuroma, you're going to have some decisions to make."

"What kind of decisions?" my mom asked. "Why do y'all keep talking about me like I'm not here? I'm right here, and there's nothing wrong with my brain. Huntsville has great doctors. I'll be just fine being taken care of there."

"No, Mom, we'll need to do all of your tests and procedures here. Your records and doctors are here now. It'll be easier if we stay in the Vanderbilt medical system. Looks like you're going to be here a while."

"I'm not moving up here. You can just forget that right now."

"I know. Let's just see what the doctors say." The other doctors had a lot to say. There was a psychiatrist, a neuropsychiatrist, and I'm sure I'm leaving someone out.

I lied. I don't know if it was the first time I lied to my mom, but it was the first time I lied and didn't feel guilty about it.

I would get used to lying to my mom. A friend of mine calls this "therapeutic lying." Sometimes, when you're dealing with a dementia patient, lying is the best option you have. It's the only way to get through the moment you're in.

I knew Mom wasn't going home. She was going to have to move, I didn't know how I was going to get her to move, but I was going to have to come up with something. There was something wrong with Mom, and the MRI on the wall wasn't going to let me forget it. What we had suspected—that something was wrong with Mom—was now confirmed in black and white. We had to deal with the acoustic neuroma first, and then? We didn't really know. Nobody did. We just knew we had some decisions to make about Mom's life, and I, not Mom, would make them.

My mom had been diagnosed with an acoustic neuroma before my dad died. As I understand it, an acoustic neuroma is a tumor that grows on the balance nerve inside the skull. Because the tumor grows on the nerve where the facial, auditory, and balance nerves all run together, the symptoms can be confusing and frustrate an early diagnosis. The first symptoms are usually vertigo and headaches. This is treated with medicine and rest. My mom tried that, and of course, this treatment didn't work. There is also a loss of balance, and finally, the hearing will be lost in the affected ear. Mom had been experiencing most of, if not all, these symptoms. They were not only growing in their intensity, but also their frequency. Mom never mentioned any of her symptoms or growing discomfort as long as my father was alive. I don't know how, but she willed herself through it. Her last MRI had shown the neuroma had grown and was pushing against everything else in that part of her brain.

With my father having died the previous April, we now had time to deal with Mom's situation. Convincing her to come to Nashville for her treatment and recovery wasn't too hard. After several tests in January, we discovered the neuroma was blocking the circulation of fluid through the brain. She had a shunt inserted to drain fluid from her brain, and after that, started radiation treatments designed to shrink the tumor. These procedures were rather minor and routine.

Her surgery to insert the shunt was scheduled for February. We planned for her to stay with us while she healed from surgery through the completion of the radiation treatments. How hard could that be?

Let's just say I asked that when I was still very naïve in the process. I was assuming we'd be dealing with my mom, but we weren't. We were part of the treatment team of a *patient*. This was the moment when I began to learn that every decision I made in my life would be made with Mom in mind. Want to travel? How quickly could we get back if something happened to Mom? Want to go out to dinner with friends? Okay, but I couldn't stay out late. I had to have coffee with Mom. Want to have a day off? Not likely. We'd probably have to take Mom to the doctor.

Normally, keeping Mom wouldn't be a problem, but we didn't have "normal" anymore. When you're engaging an Alzheimer's patient no one has "officially diagnosed" yet, it can be explosive. The MRI was only one indicator. There were more tests—a lot of them—and we would go through that process in due time, but right now, we knew, but we didn't *KNOW.*

While we knew something was wrong with Mom, we still thought we were within the assumed ranges of "normal." We weren't, and without warning, we found ourselves living through daily episodes of *The Twilight Zone.* Little things became big things, such as when we took her to the hospital for a series of tests to prepare for her surgery. She wouldn't allow them to take an MRI. Why not, Mom?

The MRI tube at the hospital was too small. The platform on which she had to lie was too hard and hurt her back. Besides, no one else had ever wanted to do an MRI, why did we want her to have an MRI now? What were we trying to do to her? Why couldn't she go home and have an MRI done in Huntsville? She didn't trust these Vanderbilt doctors. We would get her through it, but just barely. Jeannie and I would be exhausted when we got home from wrestling with Mom all day long. Wrestling with Mom would become a daily occurrence.

We knew one of the symptoms of a neuroma was incontinence. We knew Mom was using pads for protection. What we didn't know is that she wasn't throwing them away. Because she was embarrassed, she hid the used pads. We didn't figure this out until we noticed the smell in her room.

Then, the accusations began. Jeannie had stolen her stuff. Everything in our house, according to Mom, had once belonged to her. We had stolen her silver, her plates, her utensils, her sheets and blankets. Even the pictures I had of her and Dad—they were hers—we had just stolen them. We had stolen everything from her, and if we thought she was just going to stand by and take this, we were sadly mistaken. She'd call her lawyer and put us all in jail.

Did you know paranoia is one of the symptoms of Alzheimer's? I know it now. Just before she moved to Nashville, she had a new security system installed in her home. She had the security company install over ninety sensors in her house, including sensors on the second-floor windows. How did she expect someone to break into her house on the second floor?

I was ever the optimist and the last one who would believe something like this could ever happen to my mom. She was the strongest person I had ever known, and I couldn't get it through my head she was going down like this. I tried to reason with her about the security system, but she wouldn't listen. She never answered me. She just kept telling me how the neighborhood had changed. There were teenagers walking up and down the street (she lived two blocks from a school). Somebody, somewhere had gotten robbed—and I guess given the entire population of the United States, that was probably true.

Her declining condition would make our trips to the doctor even more exciting. The great thing about living in Nashville is you have access to some of the greatest medical care in the world. The bad thing about living in Nashville is you have access to some of the most respected doctors in the world, and you can't make a decision without seeing at least six doctors.

Mom was no different. We had visits with the Chief of Neurosurgery, psychiatrists, psychologists, nurse practitioners, therapists, and social workers. Every appointment we had and every expert we saw would give us one more answer, one more part of the puzzle, and create a whole new wave of paranoia.

Mom's medical file grew quickly to several inches thick.

The doctor had been right. The acoustic neuroma wasn't a problem. Her shunt was implanted, and her symptoms improved almost immediately. She regained her balance and rarely suffered any bouts of vertigo. She had to be at Vanderbilt early in the morning for her radiation treatment. Fortunately, several of the doctors were members of our church and made sure Mom got VIP treatment. The radiation did its work and over the next few months, the neuroma gradually shrunk and faded away.

Church members signed up to take her to her treatments. They would meet us at the church, go to her treatment, and then go out shopping, to breakfast, or sightseeing. Mom was treated like a queen. Those who took her to her treatments would come back to my office laughing at some story Mom had told them. They always wanted to find out if the stories she had been telling them were true.

They were. They all were. She had a lifetime of stories to share.

Anyone who met my mom loved her.

Coffee with Mom: "The only thing the doctor told me was what I already told him. Next time, I'll just go talk to a parrot."

But things were changing, and the doctors were confirming our worst fears. Mom had a problem, and it wasn't going to get better.

Mom was prescribed rehab after her surgery. Most of the exercises were focused on her balance and coordination. She did pretty well, but she wasn't always a compliant patient.

"Did you know what they made me do today?"

"No, ma'am. What did they make you do?"

"I had to walk across the room toe to heel. One foot in front of the other. Now, who walks like that? What good does it do to get really good at something no one ever does?"

"Well, keep at it, Mom. You're doing great."

But she didn't do great at everything. She couldn't remember words. In one test, she was given three words to remember. They would move on and talk about something else, and then ask Mom to recall the three words. She couldn't. Again, she had a perfect alibi.

"Why should I have to remember everything for them? If it's important to them, they should write it down like I do. I write everything down. They should learn to do that too." And she did write everything down. Her purse was filled with little notebooks with scribbled notes of things she didn't want to forget—appointments, phone numbers, people's names, and grocery lists.

And then, the big rock dropped. She failed the driving test. She was told to drive around the neighborhoods around Vanderbilt University Medical Center, and when they were sufficiently away from the hospital, the therapists told Mom to find her way back. For most of us, it would have been a simple process of determining where we were located in relationship to the hospital and driving back. We may not have taken the most direct route back, but most of us would have gotten there.

It wasn't simple for my mom. When the therapist told her to drive back, she panicked. She couldn't figure out where she was or how to get back.

She flunked the driving test.

The therapists didn't say anything when they walked back into the rehab center, but Mom barely waited until she got to me.

"These idiots say I can't drive. They say I flunked the driver's test. I've been driving since I was twelve years old. I used to drive my sisters to school and church after our mother died. I've never had an accident. I've never had a ticket. Then these educated, blue-coat-wearing idiots tell me I can't drive. Well, I'm going to drive. They can't tell me what to do. I'm going to drive. You're not going to take my car away."

I couldn't get a word in. Mom never seemed to take a breath. I got the feeling that she thought if she just kept talking, no one could tell her she couldn't drive. This was going to be a fight, and I wasn't ready for it. She didn't have her car with her in Nashville, but she would go back home soon. What would I do then?

"Mom, no one is going to take your keys from you. We still have a couple of doctors' visits to go. Let's talk to them, and we'll get all of the information together then sit down to make a good decision. Just like we always do."

I wasn't lying or making things up. We did have two more doctors' visits. They didn't go well either.

The first doctor was a nationally known psychiatrist who specialized in Alzheimer's. He was the guy who wrote the articles and did the studies everyone else quoted. The appointment was short and to the point. His diagnosis was definitive.

"She has Alzheimer's, and from her MRI films, I'd say she has vascular dementia as well. You need to start thinking about a place for your mother to live. She can't live by herself. She's going to need someone to look after her. Do you have plans?"

"Are you sure?"

"Did you know smell is one of the first senses to be affected by Alzheimer's?" the doctor asked. "That's why so many of these patients have kitchen fires. They can't smell the food burning. Your mother couldn't tell the difference between the smell of chocolate and ammonia. She failed every one of the memory tests. You need to start making plans for her."

We still had one more doctor to go. A geriatric neurologist who specialized in senior adults and their brain issues. His diagnosis was just as fast and just as definitive.

My mom had Alzheimer's, and she wasn't going to get better.

She wasn't going to give up either.

"I don't have Alzheimer's. There's nothing wrong with my brain. There's nothing wrong with me. I've just been under a lot of pressure. Your daddy was sick, and I cared for him around the clock for the last twenty years. You have no idea how hard that was on me. And I had to take care of everything. There's nothing wrong with me. I'm just tired."

"But, Mom, the doctors . . ."

"Doctors? What doctors? Those idiots? What do they know? Touch your nose, walk backward, who's the president? Like I was on some kind of game show. They didn't ask me anything that mattered. Like what bank do I go to? Where's my church, or who's my pastor? They just ask me a bunch of nothing, and when I wouldn't play, they told you to stick me in a home."

"Mom, no one is going to stick you in a home."

"You know, when my grandmother and granddaddy got old, the children just built them a little house on the farm and cared for their parents. I can remember going out to their little house to play. But children don't do that anymore. They just stick the old folks in homes and forget all about them."

"Mom, we don't live on a farm."

Then, the paranoia returned.

"I bet you've been planning this all along, haven't you? You think you're just going to throw me out of my house and steal all my stuff. Well, you've got another thing coming if you think you're going to get one dime from me. I'll dig a hole and hide it in the yard. After everything your father and I did for you. We bought you cars, helped you buy your first house, helped put your boys through college, and now, you're going to just throw me in the street. Take me home. Take me home right now. I don't want to stay here anymore. Take me home now."

"It's too late to take you home tonight. We'll go tomorrow."

"You're lying. We're not going tomorrow. You're such a liar. I wonder what your church would think if I told them what a lying [expletive] you are."

Yep, that's right. My own mother called me a lying [expletive]. She would do worse. I wouldn't be prepared for that either.

They say Alzheimer's isn't contagious. Maybe not. I just know when Mom was diagnosed we were all infected.

It wasn't just my mom who had Alzheimer's. We all did, and this journey was just getting started.

Coffee with Mom:
"Sometimes I think you guys have Alzheimer's and not me. Seems to me you're the ones with the problems. I'm fine."

Chapter 5

Taking the Car Keys

Mom and Dad moved to Huntsville in 1961. During that time, they had made friends with everyone in the city. Okay, that may be an exaggeration, but it's not much of one. They knew everybody, and everybody knew them. Everyone knew Dad had died, and everyone knew Mom lived alone, so her friends watched over her. It wasn't long before I started getting calls. They would always call me at church because, while no one knew my home number, Mom and Dad had told everyone about the church where I am pastor. Before long, it wasn't unusual to have three or four messages a day.

> **Coffee with Mom:**
> **"I'm going to buy a car. Don't worry. I'll stop by your house and tell you goodbye."**

Almost all of them began with the same request, "Please don't tell your mother I called." Then they would tell me the latest adventure caused by Mom's disease. The stories ranged from funny to downright scary. One time she showed up at her usual restaurant for breakfast at four in the morning. She banged on the door until the cooks came out and told her they weren't open yet. What made the story funny was she argued with them that it wasn't four o'clock in the morning.

I still smile when I hold that picture in my head. The cooks at this southern meat and three, wiping their hands on their aprons, pointing to their watches, and explaining to my mom it was too early to be open. Mom, of course, wouldn't hear them. She would tell them it was time for breakfast, and they'd better be ready to serve her and her friends. She'd tell them she'd been coming to their restaurant for fifty years, and she wanted breakfast.

My mom was never wrong. If she was, you'd never get her to admit it.

She started showing up at neighbors' houses on wrong days for events, and friends began to notice scratches and dents in her car. I had seen them too, and when I asked Mom about the damage to her car, she said teenagers had been vandalizing cars in the neighborhood.

For that matter, I felt I was arguing with a teenager. I knew she was lying. She knew she was lying, but she was going to see just how far she could run with it. If I challenged her, she would tell me Dad did most of that damage. The truth was Dad never drove her car. He always drove his pickup. If they drove Mom's car, then Mom drove. She never let anyone drive her car. Mom would never give up control for that long.

Her friends were telling me she shouldn't drive. Her doctors were telling me she shouldn't drive. I knew she shouldn't drive. The therapists at Vanderbilt had advised me to take the keys. The doctors at Vanderbilt had advised me to help my mother find "alternative transportation." The vote was unanimous. Everyone agreed something had to be done.

Which meant, of course, that I was the one who was going to have to do something. While everyone agreed something needed to be done, no one had the guts to confront my mom. Everyone would leave that up to me.

While everyone might have agreed that Mom shouldn't be driving, Mom vetoed everyone else's suggestions and thoughts.

Coffee with Mom:
"Have you bought me a car yet? I could have built a car in the time I've been sitting here waiting on you."

I was Mom's son. My mom and I have always had a very close relationship. Whenever my dad was facing a complicated situation with my mom, he would call me and tell me, "You need to talk to your mom."

And now, I would be the one to talk to her about her car, the keys, and the rest of her life.

This was going to be a suicide mission.

"I've been driving since I was twelve years old. When my mother died, my daddy would go to work, and I would be in charge of my three little sisters. We would drive to school. I would pick them up. I would take them over to our aunt's house who kept us. I would take them to church. I did everything, and I did it all driving. And I'm not going to stop driving now," she added. "I'm fine. There's nothing wrong with me. You just have no idea how your daddy's death has affected me. When you lose your mate, you lose everything. We did everything together, and sometimes when you all think I'm not paying attention, I'm thinking about him. I wish he hadn't died. I'm just lost without him."

"I understand that, Mom, but we're talking about your driving now. There does seem to be some problems." (I was still under the impression I could reason with my mom.)

"What problems? I bumped into a few things. Mike, you know how tight that driveway is. Your daddy used to run into things all of the time back there and you never took his keys away."

"But the doctors . . ."

"What doctors?"

"Every doctor we talked to, Mom."

"Those whack jobs at Vanderbilt? The ones who made me walk around and wave my arms in the air to prove to them I wouldn't fall over? The doctors who made me walk around toe to heel like I was a little girl in dance class?"

"Mom, they're not whack jobs. I took you to the best doctors I could find."

"Well, you should have kept looking. Those doctors asked me some stupid questions for about ten minutes, and then miraculously concluded I shouldn't be driving. Who do they think they are?"

"Mom, you failed the driving test."

"I got lost in downtown Nashville. I didn't get lost at home. I got lost in a city where I had never driven. Let me take the driving test here, in my hometown. I'll bet I'll pass the test here."

"But, Mom . . ."

That's the problem when you're dealing with an Alzheimer's patient; sometimes they make sense. Well, almost. What if we did allow her to take the test in

Huntsville? What if she was just confused being in a strange city and panicked when she realized what was at stake?

I was a rookie at doing this, and I was getting schooled by my own mother. One of her tactics was to create enough confusion so I couldn't tell which way was up. I wanted to do the right thing, but what was the right thing?

I knew I wasn't trying to take anything from my mother. I knew I was only trying to protect her, but she would throw up just enough smoke that sometimes I would end up being unsure of my own motives.

"Mike," my friends would say, "that's just the disease talking."

I knew that, but it looked like my mother.

I had to learn, for one thing, to have the plan already worked out before I started talking to my mom. If I got into a debate with her, she would create such chaos in the conversation that I would forget what we were talking about. More than once I would come home from visiting my mom, and Jeannie would ask if I had accomplished the task I went to Huntsville to do.

"No," I would say, "I didn't."

"What? Why not?"

"I don't know. I just go so confused."

"Sometimes," Jeannie would say, "I think you're the one with Alzheimer's." And some days, I thought that too.

My mom's next move was bargaining. What if she promised just to drive to the bank, the grocery store, and to church, but nowhere else? She would be careful, and she would only drive in times of low traffic. Besides, on Sunday morning when she went to church, there was no one on the road. She'd be fine.

Okay, I know what you're thinking. *Surely, he didn't fall for that one.* Yes, I did. I'm not proud, but like I said, dealing with an Alzheimer's patient, you get a little crazy yourself.

And you know what happened. The first way I knew Mom was lying to me—besides my own common sense—was a picture sent to me from my nephew. My nephew had taken his family to our family's lake house, and Mom had driven out there to see them. There she was in the picture! Standing on the deck holding her great-grandchild.

"Mom, what were you doing at the lake?"

"I didn't go to the lake."

"Mom, I have a picture of you on the deck holding your great-grandchild. How did you get out to the lake?"

"Oh, that? It was so good to see all of them. That little boy has grown up so much. He's so cute . . ."

"Mom! How did you get to the lake?"

"I drove. I just ran out there to get everything unlocked and hooked up for them. They had such a great time."

"Mom, you promised you wouldn't drive to the lake house."

"Well, sometimes things can't be helped."

"Mom, you can't be driving on the highway like that."

"Why, I'm fine. Everything is fine. I just drove out there and drove back. I don't know why you're getting all upset. Nothing happened."

"Mom, you're not supposed to be driving at all."

"Mike, you're not going to take my keys—"

"Mom, I don't want to, but I'm responsible since the doctors said—"

"Oh, those whack jobs? They made me walk around with my hands in the air . . ." And here we would go again.

There was one more incident. In the moment, it didn't seem that big. My friend meant it as a joke, but it hit me like a ton of bricks. One of my good friends is an attorney, and we were talking about our parents. He was dealing with a similar situation with his father. I was talking about my adventure in trying to get my mom to stop driving.

He laughed, and then he patted me on the back. "Let me tell you your future," he said. "The plaintiff's attorney will ask you, 'Mr. Glenn, did you know your mother shouldn't be driving? In fact, didn't your mother's doctors tell her she shouldn't be driving? But you let her drive anyway and that's when she hit the school bus' . . . And when you answer 'Yes,' they come and take all of your stuff too."

Wait a minute. I knew Mom shouldn't be driving. I let her drive anyway. I'm power of attorney. I'm supposed to act in her best interest. And now, everything I have is at risk every time she drives.

I have never been this afraid. I couldn't get the keys from her fast enough.

"You can't take my keys! I need my keys! You are ruining my life."

"Mom, I have no choice. I really have no choice."

I got the keys. I got both sets of keys. I thought it was over.

It wasn't. She had another set. So, we ended up going through the whole thing again. Once I moved her to Nashville, I sold her car, and she didn't drive anymore. Well, at least that I'm aware of anyway.

Sometimes, life gives you hard choices, and sometimes, life doesn't give you any choice at all. This is where I was. My mom was sick. She could no longer handle her life. I was going to have to do that for her. The problem was, unlike with cancer or heart disease, Mom didn't know she was sick. At least, Dad knew he was sick.

Mom felt fine, and as far as she knew, she was reading the world correctly. There was no bump on the head, and then things were different. She just woke up one morning and things didn't work the way they did the day before. She couldn't remember. She couldn't put things together. She couldn't finish a simple task. She couldn't remember recipes she had prepared for years.

But there was nothing in her body or mind telling her anything was wrong. In fact, her mind was telling her things that weren't true. She didn't lose anything. It was stolen from her. She didn't bang up the car. Some vandal had hit it with a hammer. She wasn't missing money from her checkbook; she had just forgotten to write down a check. No matter, she would say, the forgotten check would show up. When it didn't, the bank tellers were thieves.

And sooner or later, she would work it around until it was my fault. I guess it *was* my fault, or at least my responsibility. She was my mom. I was her son, and I was the one who would have to make the hard choices about her life.

That meant taking the keys from her for her own safety and the safety of everyone else. I would sell her car. If she wasn't driving, she didn't need a car. I would sell her house and most of her furniture, and I would choose the retirement center where she would live.

She would bring this up to me every day for the next four years. If we didn't talk about it every day, we talked about it the day after.

When was I going to get her a car?

When was I going to take her back home?

How could I do this to her?

What had I done with all of her money?

How could I sleep at night knowing all I had done? To be honest, at first, I didn't sleep well at all. I worried I hadn't made the right decision. I worried I was hurting Mom. Then one night I realized Mom might have been angry, but she was safe. The world was safer because Mom wasn't driving.

It might have been hard. It might have been uncomfortable, but everyone was safe, and I could live with that. Sometimes life gives you hard choices, and other times life doesn't give you any choice at all. Either way, you still have to choose and carry the consequences of that choice for good or bad.

Coffee with Mom:
"When you buy me a car, I can drive over and have coffee with you in the morning."

Chapter 6

Trusting Me to Do the Best I Can

One of the hardest things about dealing with a parent who has Alzheimer's is there's never a clear-cut answer on what to do next. Even if you know "what" to do, knowing "when" to do it is just as baffling. As a caregiver, you're constantly dealing with "on one hand" and "then, on the other hand."

Do you need to take away the car keys? Yes, I do. Are you sure? No, I'm not. So, it's okay if she drives. No, it's not okay that she drives. So, you're going to take the keys from her? Sure, I guess. But when? I don't know.

> **Coffee with Mom:**
> "So, I have to remember to take this pill that will help me remember everything else?"

Do you need to take over the finances? I'm not sure. She seems to be doing okay right now. Are you sure?

No, I'm not. I don't think she's behind on anything.
Have you checked? No, Mom would consider that an
invasion of her privacy. So, having her power cut off is
okay . . . well, no. Okay, I need to take the finances, but
how do I do that?

Do you need to increase her meds?

Her level of care?

Do you need to call the doctor?

Can I see her today, or would seeing me just upset her?

I guess. Maybe. I just don't know.

Because you're never sure, you're always running
these questions around in your brain trying to make
sure you're doing the right thing. Caring for your
patient is hard, but one of the things that makes it so
hard is you're never sure you're doing the right thing. If
you could be sure, 100 percent sure, we wouldn't mind
doing the hard things.

It's just that you're never sure.

Guess what? Mom was never sure either. She was
twenty years old when she had me. She and Dad had
been married for just over a year. I was born when Dad
was an airman in the Air Force. I was born in the base
hospital, and they charged my dad seven dollars and
fifty cents. He said later it was the best seven-fifty he
had ever spent. Even with all of the benefits the military
gave my dad, they were still broke and had no help from
their families. They were just two young, scared kids
trying to make their way in the world.

Then, I showed up.

And Mom had no clue how to deal with me either. She just got up every day and tried to figure things out. I didn't come with an instruction manual. There was no website to check. There was just me. If I was unhappy, I cried. If I was happy, I laughed. That was pretty much it. Anything else was guesswork.

I do know this, because she told me this story a thousand times. The Lindbergh kidnapping happened in 1932. For some reason, this crime was fixated in my mother's mind. Even though it happened before I was born, even before she was born, she was determined that no one would ever kidnap me. I was such a beautiful child (her words, not mine) that she was sure someone would want to carry me off. So, she never left me alone for the first years of my life. I wasn't left with a sitter. I was never taken to the nursery at church. I would sit with her.

Mom would have given her life for me. I knew that. I always knew that. Whatever her faults, my mom more than compensated for them by the fierceness of her love for me. The Bible is right. Love does cover a multitude of sins.

I simply trusted Mom to do what was best for me. There was never a meeting. We never discussed terms or expectations. It was just understood. If she made a decision concerning me, she would make that decision with only one criteria: what was best for Michael (Mom always called me by my full name).

From the food I ate to the clothes I wore, from the schools I attended to the place I went to church—all of that was done to achieve the best for her son. I didn't ask that she be perfect. I didn't demand she do everything the way I would have done them. I just wanted her, to the best of her ability, to do what was best for me.

**Coffee with Mom:
"I tried to raise
you right. I really
did, but you turned
out all wrong."**

Now, my mother was old. My mother was sick. She couldn't make the decisions she used to make. She can't do the things she used to do. Now, I was making decisions for her. The same criteria that applied to her as my mom now applied to me as her son. There was only one question: Is what I'm doing in the best interest of my mom?

> Have I chosen the best doctors I could find?

> Is the memory unit at Morning Pointe taking good care of her?

> Is she taking her medicine?

> Are her clothes clean?

> Is she getting bathed enough?

> Is she eating?

Is she socially engaged?

Have we noticed any changes?

What do these changes indicate?

Does she need a new level of care?

Questions, questions, there were always questions, and I was having to answer them. Was I getting the right answer? More importantly, was I making each decision with love for my mom?

As when I was a child, we never met about this. There was no formal signing of an agreement spelling out what I would be responsible for and what actions I could and could not take. There were no outlines restricting my access and use of Mom's finances. I had access to all of her money. There was only one question that needed to be asked: Did I spend the money in Mom's best interest?

That's it. Maybe I made all the right decisions. Maybe I didn't. Maybe I should have caught something more quickly than I did. Maybe I should have acted more decisively and with more strength and confidence. But I didn't. I simply did the best I could. With the information I had, I made the best decisions I could. Mom was simply trusting me to do the right thing.

Was I perfect? No, I wasn't. There are a lot of things I would have done differently just like there are things my mom would have done differently in raising me.

She didn't do everything perfectly. She didn't even do everything right, but I turned out okay.

I'm not going to do everything perfectly. I'm not going to do everything right, but to the best of my ability, given the information I have, I'm going to do what's best for her. She's trusting me just like I trusted her.

Coffee with Mom: "I won't tell you my New Year's resolutions. You'll sabotage every one of them."

I think she'll be all right with that.

I will be too.

Chapter 7

Finding a Place for Mom

I kept waiting for some kind of sign from heaven. I wanted a clear indicator of arriving at another decision point on the journey of taking care of my mom. I wanted a video game called "Taking Care of Mom," and when you came to a crossroads, the game would tell you things have changed, and you need to make a decision.

There was never a definitive moment on this journey. At least, there wasn't for me.

> **Coffee with Mom:**
> "If having me up here is such a blessing, I'm going to move in with you and bless you every day."

The best we could do was "it's this way if we do this and it's that way if we do that." We were always weighing one option against the other. Each one had plusses and minuses, and more times than not, we would make a tentative decision, agreeing if it didn't work out, we'd rethink everything.

One of the hard parts of this journey is you're never sure you're doing the right thing. You think you are. You're pretty convinced you are. From all you can tell you're making the right decision, but you never know. This uncertainty can become a weight on its own.

We had now come to one of those crossroads. From all of the doctors' visits, all of the neurological testing, all of the occupational therapies compiled with what her friends were telling me and what I had seen, I was now convinced she couldn't live alone.

And that was only the first decision in this process. It was also the first fight. "Why can't I live alone?" my mom would ask. She would ask the question, however, in such a way that I knew she wasn't waiting for my answer. She had already made up her mind. To her, the answer was obvious. She had lived alone since Dad had died two years before. She had been on her own since she was a teenager. She had done just fine taking care of herself, and there wasn't any reason to change now.

Besides, where was she going to move? Nashville? She didn't know anybody in Nashville. All of her friends lived in Huntsville. Her church was in Huntsville, her bank, and all of her doctors . . . what was she going to do in Nashville?

She had a home in Huntsville. This was the home she and Dad had built. She had built it just the way she wanted her house to be built. She had it laid out just perfectly with all of her furniture just where she wanted it. Where was she going to find a house like this in Nashville?

According to her, I hadn't thought this thing through at all.

Now, remember, the challenge of dealing with an Alzheimer's patient is they don't look like anything is wrong. My mom didn't look sick. She looked like my mom. She was still strong and energetic, and her eyes still focused on me like two brown lasers. She was using the same tone of voice she used when I was a child. That tone of voice that told me the meeting was finished, the discussion was over, and now, we were all going to agree to do what my mother said. .

So, I tried to reason with her. "There are a lot of good reasons, Mom, you should consider moving to Nashville. I have a good church. You'll love my church, Mom. We have great music, lots of good people, and you can get involved. We have a lot of good communities for senior adults, you can take trips with your new friends, and we have the best doctors in the world in Nashville." The Chamber of Commerce would have been proud of the sales job I did for Nashville and surrounding communities.

None of this made any difference. None at all. I was trying to reason with someone who was losing their ability to reason. I know. It looks ridiculous as I write it, but that's where I was. I had always been able to reason with her. Now, I couldn't.

I tried the family angle. Jeannie, my wife, would be there to help her. The boys and their wives were here. Didn't she want to be around her grandchildren? And soon to be coming great-grandchildren? That didn't work either.

She especially didn't want to be around me. I was no longer her favorite son. I was a stranger; someone she didn't know who was now trying to take over her life, steal all of her stuff, and kidnap her to Nashville. I wasn't her son. I couldn't be her son. She had never raised a son of hers to act like this.

After all, I was a preacher. I should know better. Didn't the Bible say, "Honor your mother"? Certainly, that didn't mean throw her out in the street, take all of her stuff, and drag her up to Nashville.

But that was the thing . . . I *was* honoring my mother. I was trying to love my mother the best way I knew how. But it didn't feel that way. Not to me. Not to her.

Whatever we did next, here's the one thing I knew: Mom wasn't going to be living by herself. In the end, she knew it too. When I finally told her, we had no choice. There wasn't going to be an argument. She was moving. She couldn't live alone, period.

Then, she started bargaining. Remember, when you're dealing with an Alzheimer's patient, they don't look sick and sometimes they're not sick. Sometimes, my mother would speak to me with amazing clarity and lucidity. She would stay in Huntsville. She had several ideas about how she could do it. Some of these ideas were good, and some of them, well, not so good.

First, she could live with some of her friends. I knew all of her friends. I had known these women all of my life. They were in the same condition, if not worse, than my mother. Like us, they were dealing with their children about where they were going to move and when they were going to sell their homes. That was a minor inconvenience to my mother.

If they were moving to a new place, then she would move in with them to their new place. If that didn't work, then she would hire someone to live with her. Lots of people, she said, had caregivers who would become part of the family. She had known "lots" of people who had done that. How hard could it be to find someone who would live with her and help her out?

I laughed when she suggested that one. My mom would have fired anyone we found. She never let anyone help her in her kitchen. She was famous in our family for protecting her turf in the kitchen. You didn't mess with her pantry. You didn't mess with her pots and pans. She didn't like anyone in her kitchen, and everyone in the family knew that.

Hiring someone wasn't going to work. Living with her friends wasn't going to work. Mom was going to have to move to Nashville. There wasn't another choice.

But you know the old saying, "the devil is in the details"? Okay, I had made the decision Mom was going to move, but I had no idea how I was going to pull this off. How would I get her in the car if she thought I wasn't going to bring her back? How was I going to get her stuff, the stuff she would need, without creating a violent confrontation with Mom?

I'd have to the think of something, but I didn't want to do this. I didn't want to do this at all.

But I was going to have to do this. Somehow, I was going to have to get her to move to Nashville.

> **Coffee with Mom:**
> "You know what I've noticed? People bring other people here, but they don't stay here themselves."

First, Jeannie and I would have to find a place for Mom to live.

I took a day off, and Jeannie and I spent all day looking at places for Mom to move—and I mean all day. We must have looked at ten or eleven places. Each one looked pretty much like the other one.

Now, I have to confess I have a problem here. When I was little, my grandmother suffered from "hardening of the arteries." This was what Alzheimer's and dementia was once called. My grandmother had regressed to the point where she no longer knew my dad. I can remember watching my dad kneel in front of his mother begging his mother to remember him. My grandmother would pat my dad on his head and tell him he was a cute boy. This would break my dad in two. This happened every time we went to see her. I grew to hate going because of what it did to my dad.

I couldn't get that image out of my mind as we talked to the directors of memory units, retirement centers, and senior care facilities. I kept remembering what happened to my dad, and now, it was happening to me. What were we looking for? A hospital? An apartment? A dorm room? Well, yes and no. We were overwhelmed by our options. Senior adult care has become a big business. The graying of America and the distancing of the American family—children don't stay on the farm anymore, they've all moved to the big cities—means there are more and more families who need safe and engaging places for their parents to live.

For American entrepreneurs, this means opportunity, and everyone seems to have a better idea on how to best care for senior adults. There are communities filled with small apartments that encourage independent living. There are neighborhoods that specialize in senior adult amenities, such as shorter golf courses and five-star chefs to prepare cuisines for the most demanding taste.

All of this, of course, comes with a price, and even the cheapest options are expensive. We were very blessed. Dad had provided well for Mom, but even with that, we were afraid Mom would outlive her resources. The burden some of my friends are bearing is unbelievable, even heartbreaking. I thank God for my dad and how hard he worked every day. The way he provided for Mom meant our decisions wouldn't be any more difficult than they had to be.

In the midst of our anxiety trying to make the best decision for Mom, we got a piece of timely advice from our family doctor. Pick the place, he said, that's the most convenient for you. Think about your day, he added. What's it going to be like trying to see your mom every day? Or how easily can you get there if there's an emergency?

Once again, I was taken aback by the realization that if this was going to work, I was going to have to spend some time thinking about how this worked best for *me*. That sounded counterintuitive. If we wanted to find the best place to care for Mom, then Mom should be our only consideration.

That's true, to a point.

First of all, we weren't deciding between five-star hotels and tents with dirt floors. All of the places we looked at were very good places. Each of them did something a little better than the others, and that's one of the things that made deciding so difficult. Mom would like this at one place, and she would like that at the other place. Some days, I wished I could construct my own place for Mom by choosing what was best from each place we looked at.

We ended up choosing the place that was closest to our house. We could literally be there in a matter of minutes. And there were times when we needed to be. Mom would have an accident with food or just life . . . and we'd have to go get her clothes to wash and bring her clean ones. She'd run out of her medicine and forget to tell us. Doctors' appointments, dentist appointments, hair appointments, going out to eat, and just visiting—I'm grateful every day the place we chose was convenient to our lives. Morning Pointe, the place we chose, was on my way to the church, and that allowed me to stop and have coffee with her on most mornings.

It didn't really matter, however, how good our plan was, Mom was having no part of it. At the beginning of our search, she and Jeannie were running errands. Jeannie thought this might be a good time to let Mom see one of the places we thought she might like. It was a brand-new place. She would have been one of the first residents to move in. It was clean and beautiful.

None of that impressed Mom. She was not going to move to Nashville. She wasn't going to sell her house. She wasn't going to move into any apartment. In fact, she wasn't going inside at all.

She wasn't going to get out of the car.

And she didn't.

After sitting for an hour in the parking lot, using every negotiating skill she had, Jeannie finally gave up and brought Mom home.

I don't know who was madder. The only thing they agreed on was they were mad at me. I had come up with the stupid plan for Jeannie to take my mother by the retirement center "while they were out."

It had been part of my plan all along, according to my mother, to steal all her stuff and throw her in this prison.

Needless to say, things did not go well.

Over and over again, I was having to learn the same lesson. I couldn't negotiate with Mom. I couldn't reason with her. I would have to do the research and make the call. I could listen to the wisdom of others. I could consider input from others, but the decision was mine to make.

The decision was always mine to make.

And I made the decision, and Mom hated me every day for making it. I had made her life miserable. She had a beautiful home. She had beautiful furniture. I had stolen her home, sold off all of her furniture, and stuck her in this prison.

"Where's my green couch?" she would demand to know.

"I sold it."

"Why did you sell it? That was a beautiful couch."

"Because there was only one place where that couch looked good and that was in your living room."

"Well, you should have left it where it was. You should have left everything like it was. Including me!"

I couldn't, Mom. I couldn't leave things alone. If I had left things alone, they would have been so much worse than they were. I know you never liked living here. I know you wanted to go home, but that wasn't an option.

Not if I loved you. So, I made the call. I chose for you to move up here, and I chose the place where you would live. I chose the church you attended, and the prayer groups you were part of. I did it.

And for four years, the time God gave me with you, you were safe and well cared for. You were loved and enjoyed by your new friends. You ate well. You were dressed, and your hair combed, and in some moments, you were still my mom.

And I can live with that.

Coffee with Mom:
"I'm glad you came by today. I'm very busy this week, and I don't have time to sit around and wait on you."

Chapter 8

The Confrontation

I love studying military history. I especially love those stories when soldiers found themselves in situations where an impossible objective had to be achieved, and yet, no one could see how it would be done . . . until someone did it.

Washington crossing the Delaware River; General Meade holding Lee at Gettysburg; the Marines raising the flag at Iwo Jima . . .

. . . and me, getting my mom to move to Nashville.

Coffee with Mom: "Did you sell my house?" Me: "No, Mom. I didn't." Mom: "Good, I'm too old to be homeless."

If you go to I-65 between Huntsville and Nashville, you'll notice two long, deep ruts along the highway. That's where Mom dug in her heels as I was dragging her up to Nashville.

In the four years she lived here, she never admitted she

actually lived here. Not once. She never called the retirement center where she lived by its name. She always called it "the prison" or "that place." She didn't move up to Nashville—she was kidnapped, brought here, and now was being held against her will.

And it was all my fault. We had the conversation a hundred times. Each time, we would get right to the point where I would have to say, "I'm making the decision and you're moving." Each time, I would chicken out. *My mom is smart,* I would think to myself. *She'll figure it out. She'll finally understand that what I'm trying to do is in her own best interest. Any time now, she'll realize that moving to Nashville, while not her preference, wasn't such a bad option. With a little time and a little work, she'll grow very fond of Nashville and our life here.*

She never did figure it out. She couldn't. Mom was sick. That part of her brain that figured things out was cluttered with disease. She couldn't reason things out. I was assuming she would work through things the way she always had. It was physically impossible for her to do so. It simply wasn't going to happen.

If Mom had cancer, we would have talked through the treatment options and made a decision together. We would have weighed the pros and cons of each process, made a decision, and then worked together to make it happen. If she'd had a heart condition, we'd have gone to doctors, gone through the required surgery if needed, and then worked through her rehab. If it had been any other illness, Mom and I would have worked together, and I would have been able to choose with confidence knowing I was doing what she had wanted done.

With Alzheimer's, you don't have any of that. You have someone who looks like your mom, sounds like your mom, but isn't your mom. She doesn't do anything your mom would do. She doesn't want anything your mom would want. As a child, if nothing else, we count on our parents to be consistent. If my mom was anything, she was consistent. If you asked her a question today, she'd give you an answer. If you asked her the same question tomorrow, she'd give you the same answer. It was one of my mom's "lovable" traits. My dad would tell everyone that mules came to her for stubborn lessons. It was an old Southern joke, but with my mom it was too true to be funny.

With all that she had lost, however, she hadn't lost any of her strength and none of her power. She was as formidable as she ever had been, and now she and I were going head-to-head. Not only was she not going to help me make this decision, she was going to do everything she could to frustrate me in making this decision. She would load up on facts. Here are the things she had done well this week. These were the places she'd been and the people she had seen. If she was "crazy" (her term for dementia), could she had done all of this?

She would call on the memory of my father. Would he have wanted this? As hard as he and Mom had worked to give me everything, is this the gratitude I show him? "Your father would have never let you do this to me," she would say. She was glad Dad wasn't alive to see this. He would be so ashamed and embarrassed to know his son had done his mother like this.

She would quote the Bible. "Doesn't the Bible say to honor your parents? Is this how you honor me? You're the pastor of a church; would you allow any of your church members to do this to their mother?" What kind of a Christian was I? Is this the way Jesus would have treated Mary? (This one was classic, and I tried to explain Mary had moved in with John, but that detail was ignored when she realized it didn't help her case.)

Then, she would just defy me. "I'm not moving to Nashville. You can't make me move. You can't do anything. I'll call a lawyer. I'll explain to them how you've stolen everything from me. I'll show them the prison you want to send me to. There are laws now about hurting elderly people. They'll throw you under the jail."

Sometimes, life leaves you all by yourself. And here I was. My mom's oldest son. I was the one to make this decision. I was the one who would decide what was best for Mom.

> **Coffee with Mom:**
> "I talked to a lawyer (she actually did), and he said to write down everything you stole from me. I'm making my list."

And I would do it all by myself.

There wasn't just one discussion. There were several. They all followed a similar path until I finally understood talking with her wasn't accomplishing anything. Once I decided what we would do, I would then just have to get it done.

The conversations would go something like this:

"Mom, we always knew it would come down to you and me. We knew you would outlive Dad. We knew all of the responsibility for your care would fall to me. We always knew sooner or later you'd end up moving to Nashville. I wanted you and Dad to move up here a long time ago."

"Why would we have done that? As soon as we moved up to Nashville, you'd be called to some big church somewhere else and there your daddy and I would be. We'd be stuck in Nashville not knowing anyone and not knowing how to get around town. You know Buster (a family friend) moved to Nashville after Addie died, and he moved back home. Besides, I would never do that to your dad. He had his friends and his Sunday school class. And he loved his doctors. I would never take him away from his doctors."

"I know, and I respect that, but now it's just you. It's time for us to take care of you, Mom. I can move you to Nashville. You'll be there with Jeannie and me. You'll be close to the boys, and we'll have access to some of the best doctors in the nation."

"I'd love to be closer to the boys, but I've got good doctors here. My friends are here. I'm not moving to Nashville."

"Well, Mom, we're going to have to do something. You can't live in this big house by yourself. The doctors have said you can't live alone, and you can't drive anymore."

"Who said I can't drive?"

"Mom, we've been through this. You failed the driving test. You can't get insurance. You can't drive, Mom."

"Those idiot doctors? What do they know? Make you walk in funny ways, and then flunk you if you can't walk all goofy. Who walks that way? I've never walked that way in my whole life. [Expletive] doctors. Who trained them anyway?

"Besides, I'm going to retake the test. They give that test right here in Huntsville, and when they tell me to drive back, I'll know exactly where I am, and I'll just drive on back. They won't take me to a city I've never been to and drive me around in circles, and then, tell me to drive back. It was a trap. It was the most unfair thing I've ever seen. If I ever see those two guys again, I'll kick both of them."

"Mom, you can't drive, and you can't live alone. We've been through all of this."

I kept thinking Mom would remember all of the conversations we had, all of the doctors' visits, and all of the results. She had Alzheimer's. She couldn't remember, and if she did remember, she certainly wasn't going to tell me.

"You haven't been through anything. You just sit there and nod your head when the doctors say this and that about me. You just lie. All of you just lie. I've been on my own since my mother died. I raised my three sisters and myself. Now, people tell me I can't handle things. I've been handling things long before any of those [expletive] were even born."

"Mom, we're going to have to figure out something."

"I've already figured it out. I'd take care of your dad for as long as God would let me. When he passed away, I'd stay here in our house until God called for me. That's the plan."

"No, Mom, that's not the plan. You're going to have to move to Nashville. You don't have a choice."

"Who made you the boss of me? I'll tell you this right now, I don't have to do anything. I'm not moving to Nashville. You can just get that out of your head right now."

"But you have to . . ."

"No, I don't. And I'm not. You and Jeannie have been planning this the whole time, haven't you? You've been waiting to get me to move so you could steal everything your daddy and I worked for. She's been stealing my stuff all along. Don't think I haven't seen her. My silver. She stole that."

"Mom, Jeannie didn't steal anything."

"Yes, she did, and I've got proof. I'm going to get me a lawyer and sue you and her both. You know there are laws about

elder abuse in Alabama. I'll have them
lock you up so long you'll be older than
me when you get out."

"When they realize I'm dealing with
you, Mom, they'll probably give me a
medal. Now, let's talk about moving to
Nashville."

"I'm not moving to Nashville. You and
Jeannie have your own lives and you
don't need to be worrying about me all
of the time."

Now, she was concerned about me. She didn't want
to interrupt my family life or interfere with my home
life. If one trick wouldn't work, the next one she tried
would.

We had finally reached the time for action. I went
to Huntsville and picked her up. I told her to pack for
a week because we had several doctors' appointments
and procedures to have done. We'd be in Nashville for
several days.

"Are you going to bring me home?"

"Yes, when we're done with the doctors,
I'll bring you home."

"You're lying to me."

"No, I'm not. When the doctors are finished, we'll head straight back here."

Of course, I was lying. I wasn't going to bring Mom
home. She was moving to Nashville and that was that.

The plan was simple. Jeannie and I would pick her
up and take her to Morning Pointe. We'd introduce
her to the team who worked there, and we would leave
her for the night. When we drove up, she thought we
were at the doctor's office, but when we walked in, she
knew we weren't at the doctor's office.

Furious? No, that would be too tame of a word. She
exploded.

"What have you done to me?!"

"Nothing, Mom, we're just here to look."

"There's nothing I want to see here. Take
me home."

"Let's just look around. It can't hurt
anything."

"You look around. I'm going back to the
car."

"No, you're not, Mom. You're going to
look around with us."

"Why?"

"Because this is where you're staying."

I can't write what she said, and she kept on saying. She never swung at me, but she balled her fists as if that was her next option. The Morning Pointe caregivers had seen this before. They expertly slid between my mom and me and said it might be better if I left. If I left, then she could be distracted by them and their programs.

We agreed and began to walk out with my mom's angry words falling on my head like hot rain. I remember pulling out and looking back. I could see Mom pounding on the door and yelling at me. She looked like a little kid being left at summer camp.

Had we done the right thing? If we had, it didn't feel right. I felt awful. She hated me for what I had done. I hated me for what I had done.

On the way home, Jeannie reminded me of all the work we had put in selecting Morning Pointe. She reminded me of all the doctors' visits and all they had told us. We were doing the right thing. No, she said, my mom didn't understand. She would never understand, and that's why we had to make the decision. Mom was safe. She was being cared for, and she would adapt.

> **Coffee with Mom:** "What did I ever do to you that you would leave me in a place like this?"

No, she wouldn't. Remember when I told you my mom never changed her mind? She didn't change her mind about this either.

Chapter 9

I Don't Want to Remember

"Has it ever occurred to you there are things I just don't want to remember anymore?" Mom's statement shocked me. Why wouldn't she want to remember? She and Dad had a good life together. Their lives were filled with friends and laughter. Both of them were successful in every aspect of their lives. Why would anyone want to forget any of that?

> **Coffee with Mom:**
> "Why are you worried about my brain? I keep all the important stuff in my heart, and my heart's fine."

She went on and described a handful of days she didn't want to ever remember again, but she described them with such detail that let me know she hadn't forgotten anything about those days. She didn't want to remember the day her mother died. "Mother had told our daddy she'd let him know when to bring the girls to her. It wasn't like it is now. They didn't know everything about cancer like they do now. They treated my mother with cobalt radiation. It burned her horribly. I remember when our daddy came home and told us she had died. I didn't know what to do. Everyone told me I had to be strong. What did that mean? I think I stopped crying and went to clean up my room. I didn't know what else to do."

She didn't want to remember when Dad had his first heart attack, but she did. "I was at home," she said, "when they called me. They told me they were taking John to the hospital. I dropped everything and rushed over to the emergency room. I could hear the doctor saying, 'Stay with me, John. Just stay with me, John.' When I heard that, I knew your daddy was dying. I felt just like I did when I was a little girl. I don't ever want to feel that way again."

According to Mom, her life would be fine if she never thought about those days again. I guess she's right. There are days that all of us would rather forget. I know there are days I don't want to remember.

I don't want to remember the look on Mom's face when I saw the dementia kick in and she didn't know what to do next. There are moments in your life you hope you never experience. You never want to see your airline pilot panic. You never want to see your doctor stumped, and you never want to see your parents, well, human.

I don't want to remember the anger in Mom's face when I told her she wasn't going back home. She was

going to live in Nashville. Her face contorted in a mix-
ture of anger, fear, disappointment, and betrayal. How
could a son do this to his own mother? Her eyes filled
with tears. Her mouth contorted in rage and her cheeks
flushed in humiliation—all at the same time.

I don't want to remember the moment I realized she
didn't remember anymore. Once, when I was talking to
her, I asked about why she returned to school when I
was in elementary and middle school. For a few years,
Mom attended classes at the University of Alabama in
Huntsville. "Why did you go back to school?" I asked
her. "What were you going to major in?"

"I was studying for the ministry," she said. "I was
going to work in the church. Then my mother died, and
everything changed after that."

Now, there are several problems with that story. For
one thing, my grandmother had been dead for years.
She died when Mom was twelve. As for going into the
ministry, no one knows where that came from. My
mother had never talked about going into the ministry.
She loved the church, but there was nothing in any conversation in any part of her life when she had mentioned
a notion of being called to ministry.

What had happened? She had forgotten. She had
forgotten about going back to school to get a business
degree. She had forgotten when her mother had died,
and she found a way to fill in the gaps of her memory
with stories she did remember. I worked in a church. She
loved going to church. She took that memory and put

it together with the moment that changed everything in her life—the death of her mother—and added all of this together to explain another disappointment in her life, a college degree she's sure she could have done but never had the chance.

That was another moment when I realized how much of my mother I had lost. She wasn't just losing her memory. She was losing her. This is the horrible reality of this disease. A person doesn't just lose their memories; they lose themselves. After all, what are we without our memories? Isn't it the shared memories that bind a relationship together?

**Coffee with Mom:
"I don't think I forget.
I think you make
stuff up that never
happened and then
tell me I forgot."**

The moments we have in common that weave our lives together? What happens when we forget? When we can't remember? What happens to our relationships? What happens to love? What happens to us?

In the movie *Eternal Sunshine of the Spotless Mind*, a couple goes through an experimental treatment to remove the memories of their painful breakup. The irony of the movie is the couple ends up back together. While the things that initially attracted them are still there, they'd forgotten the reasons they couldn't stay together. All of us think that if we could forget a painful moment in our past, we'd be so much happier. The exact opposite is true. We can't find healing until we remember, understand, and draw some kind of meaning from what happened. With Alzheimer's and related illnesses, it's impossible to find this kind of coherence in your life.

Without memories, we can't find meaning in life. When my mom was losing her memory, she started stealing things in the center. Whenever I would visit her, I would always leave with a handful of things she had "picked up" from around the facility. Some of the things came from other residents; some came from the center itself. When I would ask Mom where she got these things, she would tell me, "My mother gave that to me."

My mother, a deeply committed Southern Baptist, was now a kleptomaniac. I tried not to laugh, but it was funny at times. I could find no rhyme or reason to the things she stole. If something caught her eye, she stole it, and it became hers. A trinket that was on the table suddenly became the priceless brooch she inherited from her mother. No matter what it was, it was always something her mother had given to her.

But her mother didn't give her those things. She couldn't have. My mother had lost everything, including those mementoes that connected her to her mother. (I kept them.) So, she picked up things and assigned them a memory. She was trying to replace the memories she had lost with new memories.

And when she couldn't find new memories, I would remember for her. I would tell her the stories that gave her life meaning. I would tell her about Dad and their journey. I would tell her about her sisters, and her homes, the lake house, and her grandchildren. I would tell the stories as many times as she wanted to hear them.

It's what love does. Love remembers. If you think about it, it's what we do for each other in worship. We remember for each other. Life is hard. Life will catch all of us from time to time; and in the hard moments of life, we forget who God is. We forget who we are. So, we gather together and read the familiar stories, sing the well-known hymns, and we remind each other of the Father's love and that we belong together.

> **Coffee with Mom:**
> **"What did I want to tell you? Probably wasn't important. I'm using my brain to remember only important things."**

Perhaps the day will come when I won't be able to remember either. When that happens, I hope my sons will come around and tell me my stories. I hope friends will come have a cup of coffee and remind me who I used to be and who I am now.

Life is hard, and sometimes we forget.

But love remembers.

Who we were.

Who we are and where we belong.

Chapter 10

This Is All Your Fault

"This is all your fault," she said. "Every bit of it. You sold my house, and now I don't have any place to go. You sold all my stuff. All the things your daddy and I had worked so hard to get and you just up and sold them. You sold everything. I don't have anything. I don't have my clothes. I don't have a car. What have you done with all my stuff? How could you make such a mess of things? Why did you do this to me? This is all your fault."

> **Coffee with Mom:** "Of course I slept well. I have a very clean conscience. How well did you sleep?"

And I guess she was right. It was all my fault. I had made those decisions. I had made the decision to move her to Nashville, to sell her house, her furniture, and her car. I invested her money for her, chose her doctors and the place she now lived.

"You kidnapped me!"

"Mom, I didn't kidnap you."

"What would you call it? You put me in your car and wouldn't let me get out. You wouldn't tell me where I was going. I call that kidnapping."

"Mom, I had to move you up here."

"No, you didn't. You just decided you were in charge and I didn't matter anymore. You kidnapped me and threw me in this prison."

"Mom, you're not in prison."

"Can I go home?"

"No, you can't."

"Can I leave here?"

"No, you can't."

"Well, that's prison, and you put me here. This is all your fault."

I guess it was.

I didn't mean for it to be my fault. I didn't get up one morning and say, "My life is going too well. I think I'll just drive down to Huntsville and tear up my mother's life." Some days, I wished it was that easy. I wish there was a moment when I had the options in front of me. Kind of a "Mission Impossible" moment. "Mr. Glenn, your mission, should you choose to accept it . . ." Of course, I would have accepted it. There was never any question about taking care of Mom.

There was just never a moment when the big decision was made. There was no before and after moment—no ceremony, no handshakes, or solemn oaths. Nothing to sign. I can't even tell you when it happened. The only thing I know is that one day I woke up, and I was in charge of everything. One day I made one decision. The next day I made two decisions, and before I knew it, I was making every decision.

Mom and I had always been close. We talked about everything. She would call and talk to me about decisions she had to make concerning property they owned, stuff with their lake house, and decisions she was having to make concerning Dad's care. She may have been curious about my opinion or interested in my counsel, but the decision was always hers.

In my family, it had always been this way. To paraphrase President George W. Bush, my mom was the "decider" in my family.

Then, one day, she couldn't decide, but she would never let on like she couldn't decide. Mom had several tricks to cover her growing inability to catch on to what was going on around her. For instance, she stopped deciding what restaurant we would eat at. If I asked her where she wanted to go to eat, she would tell me she would be happy with whatever I decided. Or, she would say that she wasn't all that hungry and any place I chose would be fine. When we got to the restaurant, she would have "forgotten" her reading glasses. She would ask me to read the menu, so she could "hear" what she wanted. The restaurant would be "too dark" and she wouldn't be able to read the menu. She wouldn't want anything this fancy. She just wanted a hamburger. Or, she would just have what I was having.

Mom had enough social skills and confidence to fake her way through most casual situations. If you had not known my mom before, you might not ever guess how sick she really was. She was doing her best to keep it hidden from me. She hated people being "in her business," and she went to extraordinary lengths to protect her privacy.

But those days were over. I was stepping into her life. I was crossing boundaries I had never crossed in my life. And slowly, but surely, I was beginning to understand what I was up against.

Friends had called me to tell me they were worried about my mother. She was forgetting things. She was missing things she didn't normally miss and making mistakes my mom never made. She was missing the house payment every now and then. She would forget to move money from one account to another, and checks would bounce. She told me she was overwhelmed with taking care of Daddy—that Dad would never let her alone, that he demanded her attention twenty-four hours a day, and she didn't have time to take care of things. He would call her when she was working on things, and she'd forget where she was and what she was doing.

But now, Daddy was gone. No one was calling her. No one needed her. No, right now, she was just lost, and I had to make the decision.

Over the next four years, Mom would get lost more and more, and I would make more and more decisions. Then, one day, I was making all the decisions. What's more, everyone was expecting me to make all the decisions. No one asked her what she wanted to do. No one asked what she thought. If we were in the doctor's office, the doctors and nurses talked to me. If they acknowledged Mom at all, it was the usual niceties.

"They talk to me like I'm a potted plant," she said.

But no one looked to her for decisions. Not anymore. In time, Mom gave in to that reality. Now, she never admitted that new reality, but she went with it just the same. She would say, "I'm thinking about doing this, what do you think?" I would respond, and she would say, "Okay, let's do that."

That was totally unlike my mother. First, she never asked my opinion. The old joke, "if I want your opinion I'll give it to you" wasn't a joke to me. It was my life. My mom only respected strength. If you asked for help, that was a sign of weakness, and Mom would never tolerate that. She would never admit that she needed help either.

Now, Mom surrendered to my thoughts and decisions. In fact, she surrendered so easily that I really didn't trust it. I thought she was planning a trap for me. She was only waiting for me to get comfortable and then, BAM! She'd close the trap around me. No, I'm not making this up about my mom. I had seen her "play possum" before. I had seen her fake weakness or need to just entrap her target in their misdeeds. I won't say I was afraid of my mom, but I will confess to deep respect for her strength and cunning.

When I was a kid, when my mom would ask for my help, she would mean she wanted me to bring in the groceries, to fold clothes, or mow the grass. You know, I was *supposed* to help. Mom knew everything that needed to be done, and she knew what I could do. She would call me and give me my little piece of something that needed to be done.

Now I was making all the decisions. I was choosing her doctors. I was picking up her medications and talking to the pharmacist. I was talking to her caregivers at Morning Pointe and making sure her clothes were clean, and she had the personal products she needed. Not all these decisions are comfortable ones for a son to make for his mother, but I got used to making them.

Coffee with Mom:
"Why don't you let me preach this morning? I could tell the church a thing or two about you."

Making all of the decisions meant it really was all my fault. All of it was my fault. I moved her to Nashville. I chose her retirement center, and I chose her church. Of course, I chose the church I pastor. This means I chose most of her friends.

According to everyone who met her, my mom was witty and funny, the life of the party. According to my mom, she was lonely, hated Nashville, and she wanted to go home.

And this was all my fault . . . and I was okay with that.

What Mom said was my fault, I began to see as my responsibility. In some ways, this was a privilege. I was honored to be able to take care of my mother.

For one, she was my mother. Who knew her better than me? Who knew her stories? Her triumphs and losses? Who knew what she had overcome? Who knew her great loves and dreams? I did, and right now, I was the only one in the world who did. Once I was able to get comfortable with this, I found a different kind of freedom. Yes, I was making all of the decisions because they were my decisions to make, and because no one in the world loved her more than I did.

It didn't bother me what other people thought or what my mom said. I was the one responsible, and the blame was all mine. I knew I was the one who was going to pay the band, so I didn't feel bad at all calling the tune.

So, the question changed. The question went from "Is Mom happy?" to "Am I okay with where we are?" This doesn't mean I became totally self-centered—quite the opposite. I became the enforcer of the standard. In the time I had my dad in the hospital, he told me in no uncertain terms how he expected me to care for my mom. I was the only one who knew what my dad had said.

My mother brought this to my attention more than once. "Your father never mentioned any of this to me." No, he didn't. Mom would never let my dad talk about dying. She thought it was a sign of him giving up. But he talked about dying to me. He talked about dying, what would happen when he wasn't here anymore, and how he expected me to take care of Mom.

According to Dad, it was all my responsibility. According to Mom, it was all my fault.

And you need to know, it's all your fault too. The faster you come to grips with this, the better off you will be.

It doesn't matter what anybody else feels or thinks. It's our fault. Are you happy with the doctor? Good. If not, find another one.

Don't like the care she's getting? Find another place. I don't care what anybody else thinks or says. They aren't living with it. They don't know. You're the only one who does. It's all your responsibility; it's all your fault.

The only thing that matters is if you can live with yourself and the decisions you make. The biggest thing you can do is do what you have to do so when the moment comes when time runs out, you can look in the mirror and say, "No regrets."

Not that you would have done everything perfectly. No one does. You will look back and wish you hadn't said this or that. You'll wish you had noticed subtle changes in behavior before you did. You will be much wiser and smarter in hindsight. But don't be too hard on yourself. No one has figured out Alzheimer's. Don't be angry at yourself because you didn't figure it out sooner, faster, or better. You did the best you could, and sometimes, that's all you can do.

Yet, when it's over—and it will be—you'll have to live with yourself.

If you can honestly say whenever you had to decide or get something done, that in that moment, you did the best you could, you'll be fine.

After all, it was your responsibility, your privilege, and all your fault. When the moment came, and something hard had to be done, when love required a tough call from you, you handled it.

> **Coffee with Mom:**
> (after I said we couldn't have coffee if she moved home) "Well, maybe I've had enough coffee with you."

And it was all your fault. You'll be okay with that.

Chapter 11

What Kind of Son Am I?

I can remember driving home from Huntsville after an intense weekend with my mother. Things were piling up, and we were getting close to having to make the decision to move her to Nashville. I guess she was sensing the coming transition, and she was beginning to dig in. She had stopped answering my phone calls. She didn't want to talk to me anymore, she said. That was because when I talked to her, I was talking about her moving. She had gone through all of her reasons for staying. In my mind, they didn't come near to cancelling out the reasons she should move.

Safety trumps friends.

> **Coffee with Mom:**
> "Are you doing the funeral today?"
> Me: "Yes, ma'am."
> Mom: "Just tell them Jesus will get you through. He's getting me through."

Healthcare trumps living in the home she loved.

Living where someone was assuring her safety and well-being twenty-four hours a day certainly trumped me being one hundred miles away and worrying all the time.

But this was it. Talking was over. We were done discussing the matter, and now, the battle was engaged. She wasn't going to give up or give in. Neither was I.

Yet, on this day, I certainly wanted to. I had had it. I had been called every name in the book. Accused of the most heinous crimes and threatened with being reported to the police, being written out of the will, and beaten with a stick. With my mom, none of those were empty threats.

Who did I think I was to just walk in her house, tell her to pack, and move her to Nashville?

If I thought she was just going to throw her hands up and go without a fight, I was sadly mistaken.

My daddy would be so ashamed if he only knew how I was acting. What kind of lying, thieving son was I? Did I think all her stuff just belonged to me now, and I could do whatever I wanted with it?

"Oh, no," my mom had said. "This was going to be a war."

And I was tired of fighting it. I called Jeannie on the way home and just unloaded on her. I was tired. I was so angry and frustrated, and I wanted out. I had done my best, but I was tired of fighting Mom. I was tired of being yelled at, and I was tired of yelling at her.

If she wanted to stay in Huntsville, I'd just let her stay. If something happened—and something would have happened—I would deal with it when it did.

There was a long silence on the other end of the phone. Jeannie waited for a moment, and then she quietly said, "That's not you."

Once again, my wife had quietly, but firmly, called me out.

This wasn't about my mom.

This was about me.

The question I was answering was what kind of son am I?

We knew who my mother was. She was the oldest daughter of Leo and Velma Bustin. Her father wanted a boy, but Mom was the closest he would ever come to having a son. He gave her the nickname "Bob" (short for Barbara), and Mom learned her carpentry skills from him. Mom could build anything, understood how to build a house, and she designed three of the houses we lived in. In the others, she designed and contracted out major renovations.

My dad called me one time and told me Mom was spending too much money on one of her house projects. "Dad," I said, "Mom is going to have a project. It's either the house or you." Dad went and bought her more drywall.

Mom was the woman who had formed a partnership with my dad to take on the world. They had won. Against all odds, my parents grabbed their share of the

American dream. They were hardworking, creative, responsible, deep in their faith, and committed to their friends and community. Life was hard. Get over it. You could have or do anything you were willing to work for, and if you weren't willing to work for it, then quit talking about wanting it.

That's who my mom was.

And I was their son.

The summer after high school graduation, I got a job working third shift in a local cotton mill. I went in at 11:00 in the morning, and I got off at 7:00 in the evening. In between, I cleaned lint off weaving machines. The work was hot, loud, and dirty. I've never felt that bad in all my life. I was tired all the time. I was nauseated most of the summer. I was off schedule. I had lost my days and nights. I went to work, and I came home to sleep. I got up and went to work, and it started all over again.

> **Coffee with Mom:**
> "Tuck your shirttail in. Going around like that makes it look like you didn't come from a good home."

I wanted to quit. I wanted my summer back. "All my friends are . . ." but Mom and Dad never let me finish the sentence. They didn't care what all my friends were doing. What they cared about was raising me. I had given my word I would show up for work. That foreman was counting on me to show up like I said I would. No, I would not quit. I would keep my word.

According to my dad, I was a Glenn, and Glenns were known to be men of honor and character. The way my dad described our family you would have thought we had descended from European royalty. I was disappointed when I realized we were only second and third generation sharecropping trailer trash from south Mississippi.

My mom had taken me to countless ball games, but she always waited for me to run back onto the field before she would call me off to go to Wednesday prayer meeting. That would give her long enough to lecture the coaches, umpires, and everyone in the stands that the YMCA, an organization with "Christian" in its name, shouldn't be scheduling baseball games on Wednesday nights when Christians went to church. It would have never occurred to my mother there may have been other Christians besides Baptists.

That's who I was.

Now I was having to answer this question again. The question in front of me wasn't, "Who is Barbara?" We knew the answer to that one. The question was, "Who is Mike?" Was I the kind of son my parents had raised me to be? Was I who I was supposed to be? Was I who I believed myself to be?

Was I the kind of man who did what was right even when I wasn't recognized for doing right? Doing right was its own reward, according to my parents. No one gets a parade for simply doing the right thing. I certainly wasn't getting a parade for this.

Was I the kind of man who takes care of his responsibilities without being told? Or, would I have to be guilted and manipulated into caring for my mom? Would I care for my mom even if she didn't want me to? Was I strong enough to take her on and win? Was I courageous enough to keep fighting for her best, even when I was fighting her too? Could I do what was best for her even when, in the moment, it might not be best for me?

Now I was beginning to understand. This was no longer about my mom's illness. Now, it was about me. I was answering the question, "What kind of man am I?" Was I man enough to do what had to be done? Would I keep my promise to my father even when my mom was fighting me with every ounce of energy in her body?

I had two sons watching me care for my mother. What was I teaching them? What would they learn from me about doing hard things? Right things? Loving things?

The switch had flipped for me. Right or wrong, this was my decision to make. I was my mother's son. No one knew her better than I did. No one loved her more.

She was my responsibility. She was my privilege. I would do what was best for her or die trying.

And sometimes, I thought I was coming close to dying, but I got it done. We got her moved, although I really can't remember how we did it. It's all a blur. I've had friends who have been in combat. The way they describe the surreal slow motion of watching the battle unfold in front of them is exactly what I remember about moving Mom. I don't remember thinking. I just remember doing what I needed to do in the moment.

I would be strong enough to do whatever I had to do. We got Mom to Morning Pointe. I told her she was spending the night there. I remember pushing away from her and telling her it was decided. She was going to stay there, and she'd better get used to it. I remember driving away and looking back at her waving her arms and yelling at me as I drove off.

From that moment on, I would understand that every decision was mine to make. Others would have their thoughts and opinions, but the decision and the responsibility were all mine. Mom was going to be mad at me no matter what.

Either I abandoned her and never came to see her, or I kidnapped her and imprisoned her in Nashville.

Either I had stolen everything from her, or I didn't know where anything was.

Either I took her to the doctor or I was meddling in her business and I should just leave well enough alone.

Either I took her to church with me, or I was forcing her to go to a church where she didn't know anybody and hated the preacher (me).

I couldn't win. I was never going to win. Mom wasn't going to be happy no matter what I did. Her "happiness" was no longer the goal; her health and well-being were. Maybe I couldn't do anything about her mental health, but I didn't have to destroy my own.

Maybe Mom couldn't live with me, but the question now was, What did I have to do to be able to live with myself?

Why would I do this? Because that's who I am. That's who my mom had raised me to be, and that's who I would be now.

"Mom, pack your bags. You're going to Nashville with me."

"No, I'm not."

"Yes, you are. You have a doctor's appointment on Tuesday, and it's best if you go back with me today."

"Well, what if it's not best for me?"

"You'll adjust. Now, get your stuff. We need to go."

"When will you bring me back?"

"We'll have to see what the doctor says."

"I'm not falling for that old trick. You're going to take me up there and put me away, aren't you?"

"No, I'm going to take you to the doctor. The doctor will probably want to run more tests or make another appointment. You know how doctors are."

"Then, will you bring me home?"

"Like I said, we'll see what the doctor says."

"I'm not going until you tell me you'll bring me home."

"I'll bring you home, but we've got to go."

"You're lying."

"I'm not lying."

"Yes, you are. Once I get in that car, you'll never bring me back."

"Yes, I will," I smiled. "Remember you're going to be buried next to Dad. I'll have to bring you home sooner or later."

"I'm not going. I'll just go to the doctor here."

"Yes, you're going, and Mom, you just need to get in the car. I'm not going to change my mind on this."

"Who made you so stubborn?"

"You did. Remember, Mom, I'm your son. I'm not Dad's son. I'm your son."

"And I see where I made several mistakes."

"Well, you might have, but pack your stuff or I will, and there's no telling what I'll pack for you."

She finally stomped off toward her room like a teenager throwing a tantrum.

I could hear her talking to me as she packed.

It didn't matter. I didn't care what she said. My mind was made up. She was moving to Nashville, and no, she wasn't coming back.

That's what I had decided.

Why? Because that's the kind of son she raised me to be, and that's the kind of man I am.

Coffee with Mom:
"Of course I'm proud of you. What kind of mother would I be if I didn't raise a son I couldn't be proud of?"

Chapter 12

When My Mom Cussed Me Out

I can still remember my reflection in the bathroom mirror as my mother washed out my mouth with soap. I was eleven or twelve years old, and Mom had overheard me and my neighborhood friends talking about the new words we were learning at school. Now, mind you, it was completely an academic exercise. We weren't actually cursing at anyone. We were just talking about how you pronounce the words, what they meant, and how you would use them properly in daily conversation.

> **Coffee with Mom:**
> My mom just called someone a "ring-tailed tooter." I have no idea what that is, but it doesn't sound good.

Mom didn't appreciate the distinction.

My mom was a conservative, Bible-believing, church-going Christian. Not only that, she was a strong Southern lady. There were two forces coming to bear on this moment: first, her cemented-in-place fundamentalist Christian beliefs; and two, her concern with what the neighbors might think. I lost out on both accounts.

My friends and I were all surprised when Mom opened the front door, politely asked them to leave, and then, firmly told me to get inside. I was in trouble. Both my friends and I knew it. Mom shut the door behind her, and the interrogation began.

Where had I learned to talk like that? Why was I talking like that? Who was I trying to impress? Didn't I know language like that was the way ignorant people talked? Was I ignorant? Things had names. Body parts had names. Was I too stupid not to know what to call parts of my own body?

I didn't answer. She wasn't asking questions. She was prosecuting her case. I was guilty, and here was all the evidence she needed to pronounce my sentence.

"Your mouth is filthy. You know what I do with filthy things? I clean filthy things, and right now, I'm going to clean out your mouth with soap! Get to the bathroom."

Part of the punishment was having to walk down the hall to your own execution. I went to the bathroom knowing what was coming.

And it did. She washed out my mouth with Dial soap. I'll never forget the taste of that stuff.

I guess these days, she would be accused of child abuse. My mother wouldn't have cared. Her child wasn't going to use that kind of language even if it meant she'd have to go to jail.

There were several things that just weren't allowed in my home. I couldn't disrespect my parents in any way. I couldn't talk back. I couldn't skip school or skip church. And, under no circumstances, could I curse. There was never an excuse or reason to curse. Hit your finger with a hammer? That's no reason to curse. Get cut off in traffic? Still no reason to use that kind of language. There were plenty of words in the English language. Hundreds of wonderful words for every occasion, and I could use any of those words to express myself. Cursing was an admission of stupidity and laziness. No son of hers would ever be accused of such.

And then, Mom cussed me out. I chose the word *cussed* intentionally. There is a difference between *cursing* and *cussing*. *Cursing* means you said some inappropriate words or used some "colorful" language. *Cussing*, on the other hand, comes from the bones. This is where you're calling for some kind of divine retribution against the target of your words. You want God to do certain things to your rival in unpleasant, painful, and unnatural ways. Make no mistake, on this day, Mom was "cussing" me out.

One of the things Alzheimer's does is it puts to sleep those gatekeepers at the front doors of your mind that keep you from doing or saying things you know you shouldn't do. There are gatekeepers that make sure you don't hold your breath too long. There are gatekeepers that keep you from eating spoiled food. Then, there are gatekeepers to keep you from saying everything you feel like saying in the moment.

My mom had lost those last two gatekeepers. Whatever she thought, she said. Whatever came to my mother's mind was exactly what she was saying. There was no hesitation and certainly no filters. Then, having said what she was thinking, she had no understanding or thought of the consequences of whatever she had said. She would say something, and then that moment would be over. She would have moved on, and the next moment of her life would have no connection to the previous moment. Each moment stood on its own, independent of any of the moments around it. If you said something to her about what she had just said, she may tell you that she never said such a thing. She would have moved on.

Part of it was the illness itself. My mom suffered two types of brain illnesses: Alzheimer's and vascular dementia. While there are a lot of medical implications in all of this, what it meant for me is Mom declined much faster and much more completely than we had expected. Mom lost the ability to control the way her thoughts and words were connected. If she thought something, she was going to say it. That part of your brain that kept you from saying things that might hurt people's feelings or that might be inappropriate to the moment, well, Mom lost that. She was always blunt and outspoken. Now, she was just cruel. She was mean in what she said and how she said it, and what's more, she didn't seem to care.

Once, when we were sitting at breakfast, she looked across the room and then asked me,

> "Am I at a place that helps people?"

> "Yes," I said, "I guess you could say that."

> "Well that makes sense."

> "How so?"

> "Look around. See how fat these people are? I thought maybe I was in a place that hired fat people and helped them lose weight while they work here. Well, that's good to know. I can help some of these people."

> "Mom!"

> "What? Don't you think these people need help?"

My mom would have never said that, even if she thought it. Remarks like that wouldn't have been lady-like or Christian. She used to say, "Wouldn't you feel ashamed if someone heard you? You don't have to say everything you think, and rarely, if ever, do you have to apologize for not saying anything bad."

On the other hand, my mom with Alzheimer's *would* say such a thing. She did say these things and a lot more . . . and she said them a lot.

Alzheimer's doesn't leave a mark. For all I could tell, my mother was still normal . . . well, as close to normal as she ever got. There was no bruise. No change in her facial expressions. No pain. Her eyes still focused on me when she talked to me. Her smile still expressed

Coffee with Mom:
"There are things an adult son should never have to do for his mother, but I had to . . . and I did."

a little hint of mischief. She was, as far as I *could see*, still my mom—looking like she had always looked but saying things I had never heard her say.

Maybe I deserved the cussing she gave me. Maybe she cussed me out for good reasons. Nothing is more frustrating for a control freak than losing control, and Mom was losing control over every aspect of her life. I had control over her finances. I was making the decisions about her health care. I was choosing her doctors. I was agreeing to the treatment plan. I was even making her hair appointments. I bought her clothes and her adult diapers. There are things an adult son should never have to do for his mother, but I had to . . . and I did.

She protested. She raged against me. "You've taken everything from me! I had a nice house. I was taking care of my life, and you tricked me into coming up here, and now, you won't take me home. I don't like it here, and I want my stuff back, you lying, no good (bunch of words I can't print here)."

For a while, I would try to explain. My mother and I had always been able to talk about things. Yes, we were both strong personalities. We both had our opinions, but we were usually able to come to some kind of compromise. Okay, most of the time we'd do it her way, and I'd get her to agree to a little different timing; but now, of course, I wasn't talking to my mother. I was talking to the illness.

Everything I said, everything I tried to explain to her, was turned into more evidence that I had conspired to take everything away from her. "What have I ever done to you," she would ask, "that you would treat me this way? Did you have to steal everything? Did you have to take my home? Why would you do this to me? Your father and I gave you everything."

And they had. It took me years to finally understand how much my mom and dad had sacrificed to put me first through Samford University and then through Southern Seminary. I never had to worry about anything. I always had everything I needed—books, cars, clothes, and places to live.

Now, I was being accused of the worst betrayal. My mom was doing a pretty good job of making me believe she was right. Maybe I was a lousy human being.

Add to this the reality that Mom was scared. The other problem with the illness is it takes you a little bit at a time. Parts of your life are lost while other areas are untouched. Mom was aware enough that something was going wrong. Not only would she forget things, she was losing her ability to figure things out. Most of the time, when faced with a problem, Mom would be able to figure out a way to handle it. Now, she couldn't. She would get lost in the details. Once she had one part figured out, she would hold that fact in one spot in her mind and work on the rest of the problem. She would get frustrated, and then, she would get angry.

Not knowing what to do with her anger, she would yell at me. When yelling didn't work, she would cuss. I mean, she gave me a good ol' Southern dog cussin'. I have tried to imagine what someone would have thought if they had overheard our conversation. My mom cursing at me and me standing there like I'm watching a scene from *The Exorcist*. What demon has been unleashed on me?

I guess it would have been more hurtful if it hadn't been so funny. See, my mom didn't know how to curse. She didn't know how to put the words together. She would put the wrong words together, and what she was suggesting I do was physically impossible. Part of me wanted to correct her cursing grammar. Part of me wanted to say, "Excuse me, Mom, but those words don't go together. If you want to say that, you have to use these words in this manner."

Really? How do you give your mom a grammar lesson in cursing? There are moments you just can't match what you know to be true with the reality you're facing. I know my mom didn't curse. I know my mom would never say the things she was saying.

But she was saying them. Someone who looked just like my mom was saying things to me my mom would never say. Of all the moments I experienced taking care of my mom, this was the most troubling. I could never find a way to align Mom's language with the woman she was. I know it was the illness. I know she didn't know what she was saying, but there are some days I can't get that scene out of my head.

My mom standing toe-to-toe with me calling me everything but a child of God.

Yes, she was angry. She had lost everything. My dad was gone. She didn't like where she was living. She didn't like the food. She didn't like me. She wanted to go home, and I wouldn't let her. She had a dream about how her life would be. My dad and she would stay more and more at the lake house, and all the family would come to see them. Mom would cook, and Dad would call us around the table and tell stories.

None of that was working out the way she planned, and she didn't know why. Why wouldn't anyone do what she told them? Why wouldn't anyone listen? Could we not hear her? Could we hear her if she screamed? Would we pay attention to her if she cursed?

She had lost control of her life. There were too many strangers in her business. She hated for anyone to be in her business. She had told us that. She told everyone that, but no one listened.

Would we listen if she screamed? Would we listen if she cursed?

Everything was out of control.

She was so angry.

She was so mad she could curse.

So, she did.

And before we judge my mom too harshly, maybe if you and I were in the same situation, we'd curse too.

Who am I kidding? I'm Barbara Glenn's son. If I was going through what she went through, I'd curse too. I know I would. I'm too much like her.

Coffee with Mom: "What's there to talk about? I want to go home. You won't let me. I guess we'll just sit here and drink coffee."

Chapter 13

Mom Prays When She Plays

"I want to give my piano to Craig," my mom announced to me one day over breakfast. She was still living in Huntsville, and I was driving down from Nashville every other weekend to see her and help her with the transitions after my dad had passed away. Mom still had rental property to tend to and other business to take care of. There were things she needed done around the house—like changing light bulbs and moving boxes in the house. We had to take care of Dad's clothes and rearrange the house a little bit so his absence wouldn't be so evident.

> **Coffee with Mom:**
> "After people heard me playing yesterday, they couldn't believe it when I told them you had taken away my piano."

Then, out of the blue on this particular morning, she made this announcement concerning her piano. She hadn't moved to Nashville yet. She hadn't agreed to move yet. We were still "talking" (translated: arguing) about it. She was adamant about not moving. No way. No how. She had lived in Huntsville for more than fifty years. All of her friends were in Huntsville. Besides, by the time she moved to Nashville, some big church somewhere would call, and I'd move away, leaving her in Nashville where she wouldn't know anybody. (She threw this up to me several times. "How much longer are you going to be at that church anyway?" No matter how much I tried to explain the work I had ahead of me at Brentwood, I was always one Sunday from being called to another church.)

While she wasn't going to agree to move to Nashville yet, she was considering downsizing. Some of her friends had found some very "cute" condos, and they were very happy there. She wasn't ready to move into a retirement center. She wasn't going to give up her kitchen and have strangers cook her food.

Downsizing would mean she would have to do something with her baby grand piano. Her beautiful baby grand piano—the one she played every day. She played in the morning. She played at night, and any time during the day she could slip away from her chores and meetings, she played her beautiful piano.

And she played beautifully. She inherited her musical gifts from her mother who played and sang. Mom began taking music lessons when she was a child, and she never lost her love for the piano or songs of the faith.

She would tell me of going to singing schools in the summer and attending shape-note singings at churches in the area.

That never changed. Mom and Dad would invite friends over after church on Sunday nights, and after everyone had brought leftovers to be shared, they would all migrate toward the piano. Mom would play, and everyone else would sing. And I mean everyone. You didn't have to have any talent, just the willingness to make a joyful noise. I don't remember many people who couldn't sing, except me and Dad. Dad told people that he was the only man in the church who had been asked NOT to sing in the men's choir.

But Dad and I enjoyed the music, and Mom always brought the music with her. When she moved into Morning Pointe, she immediately found the grand piano. After a few weeks though, she insisted on having a piano in her apartment. She didn't want to share the piano. Too many of the "other people" at the residence played. One resident, she told me, thought she owned the piano and was telling Mom not to play "her" piano.

Of course, Mom played it anyway.

Several years ago, we started a young adult worship experience called Kairos. The worship experience was attended by twenty-somethings who came from all over Nashville. Mom and Dad had attended previously, and the young adults knew my parents. Now that Mom lived here, she was becoming the mother of Kairos.

As I mentioned at her funeral, if you stayed in my mom's world for too long, she became your mother. The young adults were no exception. She became their mother too. Before I knew it, these young adults would be sitting around her table talking with her and asking her advice about relationships, dating, and their own parents. Mom would sit there as long as they would.

She would play the piano for them as well. One night as we came to the close of worship, Michael Boggs, our worship leader, told the congregation, "Mike has told us about listening to his mother's playing the piano all of his life, so we thought tonight we'd let Mrs. Barbara play us out." And with that, he invited my mom up to the piano and asked her to start playing.

"What do you want me to play?" she asked.

"Just play," Michael said. "We'll catch you."

So, my mom started playing "Amazing Grace," and within a few beats, the band had her key, and they had all joined in. The band surrounded her with drums, bass guitar, acoustic and electric guitars. That night, we even had someone on the Hammond B-3 organ. The louder the band got, the louder Mom played. The louder Mom played, the louder the band got. When they kicked in, Mom got a little boost from the band and began to play as if she was afraid she'd never get to play again. Listening to my mom play with Nashville-quality musicians was a moment I'll never forget.

On Tuesday mornings, the Nurture Team, one of our women's pastoral care teams, meets to write cards, pray together, and fix flower arrangements for their upcoming visits. My mom loved being part of this ministry. On these mornings, I would pick her up on my way into the office so she could attend their meeting. We'd usually get to the office about thirty minutes before the Nurture Team started. So, if we got there early, I would ask if she wanted to play the piano. She always said yes.

I'd take her into the sanctuary or the chapel to one of our grand pianos, and she would sit down to play. She played totally by memory and always by ear. She could read music. She just didn't do it very often. She told me she needed a large print hymnal, and I bought her one. She never used it. I would put it up on the stand, open the hymnal, and press the book flat so it would stay. Then, she would play. The song she played may or may not be the song the hymnal was opened to. She would play for about thirty minutes, and in that time, she hit on pieces of every hymn she knew. "Rock of Ages" would blend into "A Mighty Fortress Is Our God." "Silent Night" would lead into "Just as I Am" . . . some of the transitions were, well, interesting. Others were brilliant.

I also noticed something else. Our staff began to notice when my mom would play. Whenever I would go get her to take her to Nurture Team, I would notice several of the staff members sitting quietly in the sanctuary listening to Mom play. They wouldn't say anything.

They would just sit quietly, listen, and when she left, they would wave to her and go back to their work.

Once, Jaclyn, my administrative assistant, went to get my mom in the chapel, and she didn't come back for a long time. When she finally did come back, I asked her if everything was okay. Jaclyn said yes, everything was fine. They had just been singing. Singing? My mom and her? Yep, she said. They sang every song in the hymn book, and when they finished that, they sang Hank Williams and Patsy Cline.

My mother told Jaclyn not to tell me they had been playing country music in the chapel.

But there was something about the way my mom played the piano. The music made you want to sit down and listen. Whatever else you were doing could wait. You just wanted to hear her finish the song. Somehow, the music brought a little peace to your life.

> **Coffee with Mom:**
> "When I play, I play the old songs. They say something.
> These new songs don't say anything."

It was then I began noticing something about Mom herself when she played. Mom was praying. The music wasn't just music, and the verses weren't just verses or pretty words that rhymed. These were the psalms of her life. These were the songs that had comforted her as a little girl. They were the songs she had sung to celebrate her faith. She sang them to remember her mother who died when she was twelve. She sang them to remember her friends who had played and sang with her across the years—Buster and Addie, Bill and Elizabeth, Charles and Mary—all who had stood around my mom as she played the piano and they sang. She played to remember when she and my dad were young marrieds, and me and my brother were little boys.

The illness had taken a lot from Mom, but it hadn't taken her music. I don't know if she could have learned a new hymn, but she never forgot the old ones she knew. These were the words she wanted to say to Jesus. These were the feelings she wanted to express to Him in prayer. When she couldn't find the words, she would find the music.

She was lost. Not the kind of lost that means you're separated from Christ, but the kind of lost where you can't get your bearings. She didn't sing about being separated from Christ by sin, but by the struggle of life itself. The darkness wasn't the darkness of evil, but the darkness of the light slowly going out. She knew she wasn't far from home, but she just couldn't find her way. So, she sang as if she was sure that if she sang long enough, Jesus would find her, and she wouldn't be lost anymore.

> Pass me not, O gentle Savior,
> Hear my humble cry;
> While on others Thou art calling,
> Do not pass me by.

Savior, Savior, Hear my humble cry;
While on others Thou art calling,
Do not pass me by.

I had heard her play this song a million times. We sang it at the end of almost every service at Huntsville Park Baptist Church. This was the song we sang during the invitation while we waited on those who wanted to respond to Christ. This was the song imploring our friends to come and know Christ. I know this song by heart.

But I had never heard it like this.

This song takes on a different meaning when the person playing is lost in the fog and isn't a sinner, but a saint held captive by Alzheimer's and dementia. There she was sitting at the piano that wasn't hers, living in a place she didn't want to live, and trapped in a life she didn't want to live.

Dad was gone. Most of her friends were gone. Her memories were slipping away. Names were lost and wouldn't come back. Friends she loved were no longer part of her life. Sometimes, words were hard to find.

But she could find the music. These old hymns said what she could no longer say. "Pass me not, O gentle Savior . . ."

I'll never sing it the same way again.

Jesus told us not to worry when we pray if words are hard to find. The same Spirit that searches the deep things of God will search our own hearts and find our prayers. What the Spirit found for Mom was music. When Mom prayed, she played the old hymns.

The music that had saved her when she was a little girl in south Mississippi; the music that saved her when her mother died of breast cancer; the songs she sang when her own father died years later; and the music that carried her through the early struggles of her newly married life trying to make ends meet on the salary of a first-class airman—that same music, those same hymns were saving her life now.

> **Coffee with Mom:**
> "Do you know what song they want me to play around here? 'Jesus Loves Me.' We're like a bunch of kids."

Alzheimer's had taken almost everything from her, but it hadn't taken her music. As long as she had her music, she'd be fine. She could play her prayers. She could sing her joys and grief. She would hum her faith and play out her joys.

As long as she had her music, she'd be fine. She could always find Jesus if she had her music.

Chapter 14

I Can't Be Dad

I saw her disappointment as I walked across the parking lot. She was sitting in a rocking chair on the porch of Morning Pointe, shading her eyes as I walked over to her. When I got close enough, she dropped her hand and let out a loud sigh.

"Mom, are you okay?"

"Not really. When I saw you walking across the parking lot, I thought for a minute you were your dad. As you got closer, I realized it wasn't him. It was just you."

I think I disappointed my mother every day I showed up and I wasn't my dad.

> **Coffee with Mom:**
> "Your daddy loved Easter. Since he's been gone, I've been trying to figure out, 'Is it Easter every day in heaven?'"

My mom and dad had one of the great romances of the twentieth century. Both had their challenges growing up. My father grew up on a farm that was doing okay until my grandfather died when Dad was nine years old. There were two sets of children. John Robert, my grandfather, had been married before and had several children that were twenty years older than my dad. My dad was born in the second group, the next to the youngest boy.

When my grandfather died, the oldest children wanted their share of the farm and forced my grandmother to refinance the farm to pay the oldest children their share of the inheritance. That debt is what put my father and his family in debt they couldn't recover from. Add that to trying to scratch out a living in one of the poorest areas of the country, southern rural Mississippi, and you have a recipe for a childhood of extreme poverty.

When my grandmother remarried, she left my dad and his little brother on their own. A family friend told their son and daughter, Carolyn, to go pick up Marshall (my dad was known by his middle name when he was growing up). He was going to stay with them a while. Carolyn told me at Dad's funeral she and her brother pulled up in the front yard and Dad had walked over to the car.

"Marshall, mom said you're going to live with us for a little while."

"Okay," my dad said. "Let me go get my stuff."

Carolyn told me, with tears in her eyes, she'd never forget the picture of my father walking across the yard to the car carrying a rolled-up paper bag.

Everything my dad owned was in that paper bag.

The local doctor hired my dad to run his gas station. Dad slept in the back of the garage. When the gas station closed, Dad would go to Laurel (the nearest town) and roller-skate. According to my dad's friends, Dad was something of a local hero at the rink. I've heard story after story about how well my dad could skate. I've even heard stories about him skating on the wall. More than one person has told me how fast my dad would skate around the rink, and then, jump and throw his skates up against the wall. For Dad, it was a game to see how high and how far he could skate before he had to put his skates back on the floor.

Again, according to my dad's childhood friends, he was thrown out of the rink more than once for skating on the wall. I've heard this from too many people to doubt its truth.

One night, while skating around the rink, he noticed a tall, lean brunette, and he wanted to find out who she was. So, he tripped her. As he helped her up, he apologized and introduced himself. She told him her name was "Barbara," and according to my dad's telling, he had accomplished his mission. He found out her name.

According to my mom's telling of the story, she decided right then that the guy who tripped her would pay for what he had done. So, she married him.

Dad accomplished his mission, and Mom was just starting hers.

Once, I asked Mom what she saw in Dad and why she wanted to marry him. "He was going somewhere," she said, "and I wanted to go with him."

Dad would find out my mom had been growing up with her own story. My grandmother died when my mother was twelve years old. She had breast cancer, and her death left my grandfather with four little girls to raise. Mom was the oldest, and Jenny, the baby, was about two years old.

My mother became an adult overnight. I don't know if my grandmother had told her she would be in charge, if my grandfather or someone else had said something in passing about my mother having to be in charge, or if my mom, with her personality, assumed she was in charge. She became mother to her three younger sisters. Whenever they got together, they would argue as sisters, and then, the argument would change to the topic of Mom being too controlling over their lives. Sometimes, she was their sister, and other times, she was their mother. This unique dynamic made for some interesting conversations around the dinner table.

When my grandfather remarried, it wasn't a good situation. His second wife was an alcoholic and caused untold hurt in my mother's family. Some of the relationships weren't restored until after I was an adult. Although this marriage ended in divorce, the damage was still deep.

I didn't know my grandfather had married a second time. I knew my grandmother had died and my grandfather had remarried, but what I thought was his second marriage was his third. He married a local school teacher, and she became the grandmother I knew.

Mom had started working at a local department store, saving her money so she could move out of her house and give her sisters a place to go. She was working at the department store when she met my dad.

They wanted to get out of Mississippi, so Dad decided to join the Air Force. They got married but didn't tell anyone. My dad left for basic training and wrote letters to my mom every day. I have some of those letters. My mom kept everything, and she certainly kept these. His letters sound like a bad country love song. One of them tells her that he had gotten his wedding ring. They were so poor when they got married they had to put my dad's wedding band on layaway.

When my mom was finally able to join my dad, they lived in a small apartment and scraped by to make ends meet. They were trying to start their lives on an airman's pay. I have one of Dad's original W-2s that shows they were living on less than $4,000 a year.

I don't know how they made it, and when I talked to my parents about it, they didn't know how they made it either. Dad always hustled, and Mom was always behind him. Dad worked two jobs for most of my life and three jobs for part of it. Mom would hold the house together, so everything would be just right when Dad finally got home. They didn't have much in the world besides each other, and each was determined to always be there for the other. They weren't just close, they were inseparable.

Why am I telling you all of this? Because you can't know my mom if you didn't know my dad. They lived for each other. His dreams were hers, and her dreams were his. Whenever they would get involved in a project, they would define success in terms of what the other wanted. When they built their house, Mom made sure there were things in the house Dad wanted. When I talked to Dad, he would tell me he didn't care where he and Mom lived, but the house was important to her, so he went along.

> **Coffee with Mom:**
> "I dreamed about your father last night, and I kept my eyes closed as long as I could. I didn't want the dream to end."

If you asked Mom why it mattered, she would say it was important to Dad. If I asked Dad, he would tell me it was important to my mom. I could never get a straight answer from either of them. Maybe it was because they had been through so much together. Maybe it was because they had achieved so much together.

Then, my dad had his first heart attack, and not only did everything change for Dad, it changed for Mom. Her life now focused on taking care of my dad and making sure he was healthy and lived without stress. If something upset my dad, my mother decreed we would not talk about it. If the doctor said my dad was to walk three miles a day, he walked three miles a day—not one step more and not one step less.

Mom kept my dad alive through another heart attack, another bypass surgery, numerous rehabs, and countless trips to the doctor's office and emergency room when the pacemaker or medicine would get out of whack. The last two years of Dad's life, my mother didn't sleep. She would nap on the couch in between my dad calling for her. She was his caretaker twenty-four hours a day and living on the ragged edge. One of the reasons I had such a hard time accepting her illness was knowing what caring for Dad had taken out of her.

She wouldn't let anyone help. This was her job to do, and if my dad wasn't living, she didn't want to live either.

When Dad died, Mom lost her reason for living. And no matter how hard I tried, I couldn't give that back to her.

I could do a lot of things for Mom. I could make sure she was safe. I could find her the best doctors possible. I could make sure she was fed well and had her medications. I could make sure she had nice clothes, but no matter how much I did, the one thing I couldn't do was be my dad.

I could take her places. I could talk about our children, grandchildren, and great-grandchildren, but as soon as the conversation would lag or as soon as she saw something that reminded her of Dad—and everything reminded her of Dad—she would drift off into her grief, or she would start to cry and tell me how much she missed him.

Mom did everything she could to keep my dad's memory alive. She laminated every piece of paper that had anything to do with my dad. And I mean EVERYTHING—routine business letters, travel expense reports, doctors' letters, and curriculum notes from his teaching with the Army. Everything my dad touched, anything he wrote on, anything that was addressed to him, was laminated for history.

Dad had lived a significant life, and Mom was going to make sure everyone knew it.

"I'm always amazed," she said, "at how much your dad was able to accomplish after starting with so little."

Compared to my dad, I was a disappointment.

"Mom, you were part of that team. Dad used to tell me he couldn't have done what he did if it weren't for you. Mom, you did the hard work. Dad couldn't fire anybody. If someone had to be fired from the store, you fired them."

"Your daddy was a big old softie." That would bring up another story about Dad and how he helped someone out and changed their life. At my dad's funeral, we stood in line for over five hours and listened to person after person telling us how Dad had saved their life. When we got in the car to go home, Mom asked me, "Where were we when your daddy was saving all of these lives?"

"We were in the car, Mom, blowing the horn and yelling at Dad to come on."

When you're caring for your parent, you're tempted to try to fill every hole in their life. You want to make sure they have plenty of friends and have exciting trips to take, but no matter how hard you try, there will be things in their lives you simply won't be able to replace.

When my mom moved to Nashville, or rather, when I kidnapped her and stuck her in this prison, she lost friends she had for fifty years. She lost her favorite places to eat, her hairdresser, and her favorite grocery store. She lost her pharmacists and neighbors she loved. She lost her Sunday school class and her favorite choir. She lost the geography of her life. I might as well have taken her to another planet.

Coffee with Mom:
"I miss your dad. He brought all of the color to my life. Without him, everything's just black and white."

And she had lost Dad. The one person she could always count on. She lost the person who knew her better than anyone. She lost her stories, her history, and her confidence that she could handle the future.

Yes, I look like my father, but I wasn't him. She had lost a lot, and while I could replace some of it, I couldn't really do anything about the missing parts that mattered most to her. There are some failures in life you just can't fix.

Chapter 15

You Have No Right

As I've mentioned before, my mother was one of the strongest women I've ever met. For her, it was always about strength. If she thought you couldn't handle the moment, she would push you aside and take over. Weakness was a sin. She was strong enough to get the job done, and if you couldn't, then she would push you out of the way.

And for the longest time, Mom couldn't understand how things had been reversed. She wasn't in charge anymore. I was. There was never a meeting when we transferred power from her to me. There were never any documents signed or a legal fanfare celebrating the transfer of power.

> **Coffee with Mom:**
> "What did you do with all of my clothes? They're too big for Jeannie. Are you wearing them?"

Just one day, I was in charge. I knew it. I think Mom knew it, although she never admitted it.

"What right do you have to do this to me? You've stolen all of my things. The things your daddy and I worked for, and you just came in and took them. You took everything. You kidnapped me and stuck me in this prison. What did I ever do to you that you would treat me like this?"

Those were the tame conversations. Sometimes, Mom would sound like her old self. I would recognize the tone of her voice. I could follow the line of her reasoning, but these times grew further and further apart. I soon learned that I would have to carry both ends of the conversation.

Yet, just because my mom was ill didn't necessarily mean she was wrong. Had I overstepped my bounds? Had I usurped an authority that wasn't mine? Did I have the right to do what I was doing?

Legally, I did. Mom had signed all of the papers making me her legal representative and guardian. I'm sure she didn't have this circumstance in mind. Her grandmother had lived well into her nineties. Her father had lived a long life, despite being a serious smoker for most of his life. They had enjoyed reasonable health most of their lives.

When her grandmother could no longer care for herself, the family took care of her by keeping her for six weeks at a time. I can remember taking my great-grandmother to the airport and watching her plane take off. Those were the days when you could walk with the passenger directly to the gate. I can still remember watching my great-grandmother waving from her seat as the plane taxied out for take-off. I would often tease Mom that I was going to buy her some white gloves and a little pill box hat like my great-grandmother used to wear and send her off on the next plane out.

I think she would have gone, and I guess that's why I didn't push it.

Things were turning out very differently for my mom. She was still in great health. She was strong and took very little medicine. We were told over and over again that my mom could live for a very long time. My mom had planned to live a very long time.

And she didn't plan on living like this. She was going to live in her home in Huntsville. She was going to get up every day and go eat breakfast with her friends at Gibson's Bar-B-Q. (Don't smirk about eating breakfast at a barbeque restaurant. It's the best breakfast in Huntsville.) Then, she would run her errands, and after going to the bank or visiting a sick friend, she would come home and work on her projects. She would make baby blankets, bake for her neighbors, and watch craft shows on television. She might read a little bit before she went to bed or watch a little TV, but this was her day.

And tomorrow would be just like it. This would have been her life.

I had taken all of that away from her. I had taken her car away. I had moved her to Nashville. I had taken away all of her friends. Did I have that right? Sure, I know I hadn't done any of this. The illness had robbed Mom of the life she'd wanted. Mom didn't see it that way. She never saw it this way. *I* was the one who had done all of these things. She wasn't sick. She had been robbed, and she had been robbed by the one person she should have been able to trust the most—me.

Which brings us back to our original question: *Did I have the right to do what I was doing?*

Here's what I knew. All of her doctors, her friends, and family agreed she could no longer live by herself. I had enough evidence to make a case. She had missed her house payment. She was showing up at places at the wrong time. She was getting lost driving around town. It wasn't so much that she got lost as it was she suddenly couldn't remember where she was going or why she was driving in the first place.

> **Coffee with Mom:**
> "Santa came to see us, and I told him the only thing I wanted from him this year was a ride home."

One doctor told me my mom could probably operate a vehicle reasonably well enough, but with her illness, she'd wake up one morning, and it would be that day, only ten years ago. She would have gone to the places trying to do what she was planning to do ten years ago. If my dad had been in the hospital ten years ago, she would have gone to the hospital to see him. If she remembered going to the cleaners ten years ago, she would have gone to pick up her dry cleaning in the building where the cleaners was located ten years ago.

Have you ever read stories about Alzheimer's patients trying to "break into a home"? This is what happened. They wanted to go home, and they went to the home they were living in on the day they are now remembering.

The car had little dents and scratches she couldn't explain. But these were nothing to worry about, she said. After all, didn't I have a few bumps and dings in my driving history?

I couldn't run my own life, she said, what made me think I could run hers?

I didn't want to run her life. I wanted her to have the life she wanted. I wanted her going to breakfast with friends, singing in church, making her crafts, and tending to her property and projects. I didn't want her sitting at a table staring at pieces to a puzzle she'd never be able to put together.

My mom was never declared "incompetent" to handle her affairs. I didn't have any legal papers giving me custody of Mom's business and medical affairs. I had no judge's ruling granting me sole authority for her financial and healthcare needs. She had granted me power of attorney. I was authorized to write checks, speak to her doctors, and handle her property. I was listed as next of kin in all of her paperwork and HIPAA. I knew the details of her affairs and healthcare. I was the one who people in her life communicated with.

I guess had she pushed the issue she could have
made a legal scene. But Mom had taught me to keep
good records—and copies of everything—so, I was prepared, if asked, to present the evidence that one, everything had been spent for Mom's benefit, and two, her
resources were being used in a reasonable and expected
way.

More than once, people would tell me how good
it was to see someone love their mother the way I was
loving her. Hearing that remark would always surprise
me. I didn't see myself doing anything out of the ordi-
nary. I took her to her doctors' appointments. I made
sure her clothes were cleaned, and her bills were paid. I
would argue with her about where she was staying and
convince her to stay one more night.

What else would a son do? Yes, I know there are
a lot of broken families, and my story isn't normal for
most people, but it was normal for us. This was the
way I had seen my mother and father love each other all
my life. This was the way my mom had loved me. She
had always been fierce in her love and protection of me.
Now it was my turn to love her the same way.

And I did love her. Whatever failings she might have
had—every parent has them—she always loved me. She
may have been too strict and too demanding in some
ways, but she had always loved me. I never doubted
that. In the big scheme of things, my mother's failures
added up to nothing more than style points.

I loved her. I really did. I loved her strength. I loved her biting wit. I loved the way she would confront people who were wasting her time or not handling a situation in a professional manner. I loved the way she could walk into a chaotic situation, immediately size it up, and then, in a matter of a few seconds, determine a course of action, and everyone in the room would follow her directives.

One of their friends used to say if he ever got in trouble, don't send my dad. Send my mom. Dad would come and console you. Mom would get you out of the mess you were in.

I was the one who loved her, and that's what gave me the right. I was the one she had been training all of my life to be prepared for situations just like this. I was the one she knew would do something when something needed to be done. She had raised me to do the right thing even when doing the right thing cost you something. I would do things exactly the way she would have done them, and I wouldn't really care what anyone else thought about how I was handling the situation. She was my mom. I was her son. It was my call to make.

Sometimes, my mom would get anxious. Something would happen, and she would become afraid. In those moments, she would panic a little. Her panic would be about me. Could I handle her in this moment? Was I strong enough? Remember, my mom only respected strength. If I was going to handle things, I would have to prove to her I was strong enough to do it. In fact, I'd have to do it over and over.

In those moments, Mom would bull-rush me. She would, without warning, turn and verbally attack me. She would accuse me of felonies and misdemeanors. I would be called a liar and a thief. I would be called stupid and incompetent. She was never physical, but she was just short of taking a swing at me.

I learned to hold my ground. I learned to stand there and not give an inch. I stood there and reminded her, this is where we were, and this is what we were dealing with. These were the decisions we had made, and we were sticking to them. We weren't going back, and we weren't talking about it anymore. The decision had been made, and the decision was final.

When she realized she couldn't change my mind and when she knew I wasn't going to back down or be intimidated by her threats, she would relax. She would be convinced, at least for a little while, I was strong enough to take care of her.

And I would.

And I did.

She was my mom. I was her son. I had the right to make every decision I made, because right then, there was no one on earth who loved her more than I did.

I had every right to do what I did. Love not lived isn't love at all. Love doesn't give you the option to do nothing.

Yeah, I know I made her mad just like she made me mad when I was little. Now, I was making her mad because, like her, I was insisting we do the right thing.

Somehow, I thought she'd understand.

Coffee with Mom:
"Everybody says you write stuff on me. What do you write about me? Whatever it is, I know you're not telling the truth!"

Chapter 16

Take Me Home

Morning Pointe is a very nice retirement and memory care center. For Mom, Morning Pointe was a prison from which she would soon be paroled.

"Are you taking me back to the prison?" she would ask. "Are we going back to 'that place'?" She would always sigh deeply as if she was being marched down the hall to the "Song of the Volga Boatman."

"When are you going to take me home?"

Morning Pointe was never home. Nashville was never home. When she said she wanted to go "home," she meant Huntsville. Not only did she mean Huntsville, she meant Huntsville when my dad was still alive. She may have meant she wanted to go back to a time when I was still a little boy. She

> **Coffee with Mom:**
>
> "I'm going to move back home. I'm just waiting for the right time. When I leave, I'll leave a message."

wanted to go back to a time when Huntsville was growing, but not yet big. She wanted to go to church and see her friends. She wanted to take me to school where she knew my teachers. She wanted to know the server who brought her coffee. She wanted to know her grocer and her dry cleaner.

She wanted to go back to a place that didn't exist anymore. I couldn't take her "home." Home wasn't there anymore.

I could take her to the house where she and Dad used to live, but she wouldn't recognize the house. The new owners have redecorated it. The kitchen isn't the same, and the groceries in the pantry are arranged very differently. The television is on another wall, and Dad's chair isn't there.

Dad isn't there either. The garage where she stored all of her stuff (Christmas decorations, Easter decorations, craft paints, and material) now holds three cars. Mom and Dad never put their cars in the garage. Mom wouldn't recognize anything. Everything would be so different.

I could take her back to the lake house, but she wouldn't recognize it either. It's been redecorated as well. Mom decorated the lake house by shopping at Goodwill and other thrift stores. Besides the beds, there wasn't anything in the house that cost more than five dollars. If her grandchildren broke anything, she wasn't going to get mad about it. She wasn't going to spend all of her time at the lake yelling at her grandchildren. If the grandchildren sat on the couch in their wet bathing suits, no problem. We'll just go to the nearest thrift store and buy another one. When they came to the lake, everyone was going to have a good time.

Those grandchildren are in their thirties now. They're married with children of their own. They won't be coming to the lake for Christmas. We won't be there for the Fourth of July, Memorial Day, or Labor Day. The children won't be standing around the kitchen waiting for the ribs to be pulled off the grill or biscuits to come out of the oven. We won't be sitting at the table listening to Dad tell stories or taking boat rides as the sun sets on the river.

That's all gone. There's no home to take her home to. My elementary school is still there, but Mr. Dubose, Mrs. Snider, and Mrs. Stevens aren't. My middle school is gone, and my high school has closed. Huntsville Park Baptist Church is still there. University Baptist Church is as well. But there aren't many people there that Mom and Dad knew. Everything's changed.

I'm still here, but I'm the wrong me. She wants her son with her, but she wants me as a little boy. She wants me to crawl up in her lap and read a book with her. She wants to sing with me while I'm crawling into bed. She wants to make sure I've brushed my teeth and I've eaten all of my vegetables. She wants Dad in his chair, and my brother and I on the floor in front of the TV with her working on some project on the couch. That's what she wants when she tells me to take her home, but all of that is gone.

All she has are her memories, and now, she's losing those. It's one thing to have to let go of life and go through the normal grieving process. It's quite another to have to let go of your life and forget all that you're losing when you let it go.

> **Coffee with Mom:**
> "I just want to go home. This place is fine, but it's not home. None of my friends are here. I just want to go home."

As I recognized Mom was unable to remember fewer and fewer things, I started remembering for her. I would tell her stories. We would laugh as we recounted details of our family's journey and adventures. When I stopped telling the story, Mom would fade away again. She couldn't remember what we had just talked about. She couldn't remember that she had remembered.

But for that moment, Mom would come alive again. She would be my mom, and even if it was for just a few seconds, she would be her old self again.

I began coming to Morning Pointe to see her with several stories in mind.

"Hey, Mom, do you remember our house on Pinedale Drive?"

She would smile like she did.

"Do you remember when Dad backed into the tree in the front yard? He got in his old VW van, hit the gas, and ran his van halfway up that tree. Dad got out of the van like the tree had just appeared there overnight."

Mom and I were both laughing.

"You used to get so mad at us," I said, "because we always played ball in our front yard and tore up the grass."

"And all the shrubs and trees," she said. She remembered. She didn't remember for long, but she remembered for that moment.

"Your dad used to love to walk Barney," Mom would say. Barney was their dog. He was a black schnauzer Mom got for Dad after his first heart attack. Dad loved Barney and walked him every morning and every night. That was twenty-five years later. Barney never lived on Pinedale Drive. Mom had forgotten that.

"When you built the house on Locust Avenue, do you remember how Dad would sit out in the front yard and watch the construction?"

Mom smiled. "The workers called him 'Sitting Bull.'"

"Yeah, that's right," I said.

"I miss your dad," she would say, and then, she would drift off again. Sometimes she would come back to the conversation, and sometimes she wouldn't.

Mom could remember. She just couldn't remember by herself. If I was there and told a few stories, she would remember, and she would live in that moment again. It would last only a few minutes, but she would recapture that moment. The next day, I might tell the same story again, but it wouldn't matter. She would remember like it was the first time she had heard the story.

And we did that over and over and over. I would tell a story. Mom would remember. Then, she'd forget. I'd tell a story, and she would remember. And then, forget again.

And with my family, I always had plenty of stories. There were stories about growing up in Mississippi and going to school in Laurel, Mississippi. There were stories of being in the Air Force and living on base. I would remind her that I got lost on one of the bases, and when the mailman brought me back home, she squeezed so hard I thought she was going to choke me. Then, she spanked me for going somewhere I wasn't supposed to go.

There was the story of Hazel falling out of the car, Austin and his Pall Mall cigarettes, PaPa and his golfing, Mom and her three sisters. There were stories about moving to Huntsville and paying ninety-five dollars a month for their first house payment. Mom said it scared her and Dad to death. There were stories of the television store and politics, church friends, and neighborhood gatherings. I had a lifetime of stories, and I told every one of them to her.

She would remember. Then, she would forget, but for that moment, she was home.

This was the way I took her home. We went everywhere. We went up and down Memorial Parkway. We went to the new mall and the old mall. We went from Drake Avenue all the way to Mastin Lake Road. We went from Corman's Bakery to Michael Restaurant, from Huntsville Park Baptist Church to the Jesus mosaic on the front of First Baptist Church. We would drive down through neighborhoods where their friends had lived. We drove through Redstone Arsenal. We went back to her home in Mississippi. Back to the little church in Shady Grove where she learned to play the piano. We went everywhere in between.

> **Coffee with Mom:**
> "I wish I had something exciting to tell you, but we just sat around and looked at each other today."

Every morning I would take her home. We couldn't drive there anymore, but we got there just the same. We found out we could go a very long way on two cups of coffee.

Chapter 17

The Only Man Who'll Need Two Votes to Get into Heaven

My mom cared for my dad twenty-four hours a day, seven days a week. Her entire life was focused on keeping my dad healthy. Then, as he weakened, she focused on keeping him comfortable, and finally, she put her full energy into just keeping him alive. She wouldn't let him stay in bed, no matter how bad he felt. He had to get up, get his shower, and get dressed. She usually had their day planned. There would be errands to run, people to see, and projects to accomplish.

> **Coffee with Mom:**
> "I'm glad your daddy's not here. He would hate to see me like this."

When I mentioned to her that she may be pushing Dad too hard, she told me she couldn't let him give up.

Which to her meant she couldn't let Dad give up anything because if he gave up anything, Dad would soon
give up everything.

Every day would be the same. Mom would get up,
get dressed, and start telling Dad to get up and get
dressed. Their friends would be waiting on them at
Gibson's. They had a lot to do. The rental property
needed looking after, they had to go to the bank, and
to the post office. (I think Mom made things up so Dad
would have something to do.)

Several times Dad would call me in the middle of the
day. When I would ask what he was doing, he would
wander around in his answer. Finally, I would interrupt.
"You're in the Walmart parking lot, aren't you? You got
bored and called me."

"Yeah, I am, son. You know your mama."

Whatever anyone else may think about my mom's
hard-driving style, I'm firmly convinced she kept my
dad alive longer than anyone thought possible. This was
confirmed in a conversation I had with the doctor who
had treated Dad during his first heart attack.

"I didn't think he had five years left," he said, "but
he made a liar out of me."

Dad lived twenty years after his first heart attack.
Probably because my mother wouldn't let him die.

And she wouldn't leave him alone either. If Dad was
in the hospital, Mom was in the hospital. If Dad had a
doctor's appointment, Mom was right there with him.
Every once in a while, Mom would have something she

couldn't get out of or couldn't postpone. Sometimes, strain would finally catch up to her and wear her down. Only after failing at every attempt to change things, only then, would she give in and finally go home to rest.

In those rare moments, I would have the chance to talk to Dad. I asked him one time if he had had the chance to go to college, where would he have gone? He told me LSU. That surprised me. I thought, being from Mississippi, he would have said Ole Miss. Nope, he said, in that part of the country (south Mississippi) anybody who was anybody had gone to LSU.

"What would you have majored in?" I asked.

"Law," he said. "I'd have been a lawyer, and I would have run for office." He looked at me and pointed his finger for emphasis. "I'd have been a senator," he said. He probably would, and he would have been a good one. Mom would have made sure.

I asked him if he had thought about making the Air Force a career. "Yeah," he told me, "I did. Then I found out my next station was going to be Greenland."

"Greenland? What's in Greenland?"

"A big radar installation. They wanted me to go up there and run that thing. I just didn't see a future up there. Too cold for me."

And we would talk about death and dying. Mom never would let him talk about dying. For her, it was a sign of giving up. So, Dad learned to wait until Mom was out of the room, and as soon as she left he would start talking to me.

"Mike, son, the handwriting is on the wall. I'm not going to make it much longer."

"Dad, don't say that. The doctors say you're doing fine."

"What they're saying, son, is I'm doing fine for a man in my condition, and my condition is dying."

"Are you scared?"

"No, I'm not scared of death. I'm scared of dying. Will dying hurt?"

"I don't know, Dad."

"Will it hurt like my first heart attack? I felt like someone was beating me in the chest with a sledge hammer. I don't want to hurt like that again."

"I'm sure, when it comes time, the doctors will do everything to keep you comfortable."

"I'm okay dead. I just don't want to die."

"I guess that makes sense."

"Now, son, I won't be here to make sure things are done right. I'm counting on you to take care of your mother. Now, I want her taken care of the way I would take care of her, you understand?"

"Sure, Dad. I understand."

When my dad was angry or tense, the muscles in his jaw would ripple from back to front and then back again. His jaws were in full motion. (When we were kids, this was the sign from Dad that we had gone too far.) He would also point directly at your face to make sure you were listening.

And I was listening. I got every word. I didn't have to write anything down. He burned it into my brain. "Your mama should have plenty to live on. There's the lake house. It's paid for. There's the rental property. Get what you can for the land in Mississippi, and she'll have a little from my retirement and social security. So, she should be okay. Now, you know how I want her treated. Keep her in the house as long as you can. She loves that house. But whatever you do, you know how I want her treated. You know how I want things done."

Coffee with Mom:
"Don't think I'm not going to tell your daddy everything. And when I do, you're going to be in big trouble."

I did know. The problem was Dad never mentioned any of this to Mom. Nothing about the finances.

Nothing about the property. Nothing about the responsibility he put on me.

Nothing.

"Mom, I'm only doing what Dad told me to do."

"When did he tell you? I never left his side for twenty years. When did you and he have these deep conversations about what he wanted done?"

"Whenever I would stay with him, Mom, this is what we'd talk about. He left me very specific instructions on how he wanted things done."

"Well, he never talked to me."

"You wouldn't let him. Anytime he would talk about dying, you would change the subject. Dad never got to talk about what he wanted to have happen when he wasn't here."

"But, Mike (yes, she's changing the subject), I couldn't let your dad think about dying. He would give up, and if he ever gave up, he wouldn't have lived through the night. I just couldn't let him give up. It was his will to live that kept him alive.

Not his heart, it was his will. Your dad was a very strong man."

"And your will. You're a strong woman, and Mom, I'm going to take care of you. Dad gave me the plan, and you're going to be fine. You took care of Dad for a long time, Mom. Now, it's my turn to take care of you."

(And she would change the subject again.) . . . "I don't want you to take care of me. I don't need you to take care of me. I'm fine. I can take care of myself. I've taken care of myself since I was fifteen years old. (Her age would always change. Sometimes it was fourteen. Sometimes it was fifteen.) I ran the business when your daddy was running around with his politics. I ran the house. I raised you and your brother. And now, all of a sudden, I'm helpless. There's nothing wrong with me. There's nothing wrong with my brain. There's nothing wrong with me at all. I'm just tired. I miss your dad.

"You just wait until your wife dies. You'll forget a lot of things too."

For me, this was always part of the problem. In the beginning, I could never tell the difference between

Mom's grief and her disease. Grieving people forget things. Grieving people get depressed and cry a lot. Grieving people get angry when little things go wrong, and grieving people yell a lot at people they love.

And so do people with Alzheimer's.

My dilemma was complicated by the inconsistency of Mom's behavior. One day I would visit her and she would be fine. We'd have a great day together. I would drive home thinking maybe we were going to be okay. The next time I would be with her, her behavior would border on the bizarre. We would run errands, and she would forget why she was going to the store in the first place. Dishes would be piled up in the sink, and food from several days ago would have been left out on the counters.

I would find tools in the refrigerator, and bills stuck in books on the bookshelf. She had stuff everywhere. I told her she was one box away from an episode of *Hoarders*. She kept everything. Old magazines, newspapers, paper plates and cups, every scrap of cloth her hands touched were piled into her sewing room. She had tax forms from twenty years ago. She had bills from other houses they had lived in, and files and files from the family business, even though the business had been closed for years.

She had glass jars filled with buttons, nails, screws, and all kinds of knicks and knacks. She had jackets and shirts, pants and sport coats piled on multiple beds throughout the house. Whenever I would volunteer to help her clean things up or clear things out, she would brush me off and tell me she was working on it.

If I pushed her about it, she would get angry. "Don't touch my stuff! I need my stuff! I've got projects I'm working on. I know what I'm doing. And if you're going to sit here and tell me what to do, you can just go back to Nashville."

I would go back to Nashville, but I couldn't stay there. Mom needed me. She may not have admitted that she needed me, but she needed me. And I would be there for her. Just like she had always been there for me.

My mom was a fierce mama bear. She would protect her cubs against all odds. Once, when I was a kid, an older kid pulled a knife on me. Mom exploded out the back door of our house. (She had been watching me from the window over the kitchen sink.) I still laugh when I remember my mom chasing that kid down the street promising what she was going to do to him when she caught him.

Once, when my brother got in a little trouble, my mother dressed up in her fanciest suit, grabbed her briefcase, and marched into the courthouse demanding to see the sheriff. Everyone in the place assumed she was a lawyer. Now, she never told anyone she was a lawyer. She just never corrected their assumption. She met with the sheriff, and well, let's just say she cleared up the misunderstanding involving my brother.

That was my mom. She handled things. She took care of people. Now, it was my turn. She needed me.

I needed to be there. Now, she would never admit that she needed me. Nor would she ever thank me for whatever I did. Whatever I did was what I was supposed to do, and you don't get a prize for doing what you're supposed to do in the first place.

When I was little, I counted on Mom to do what was best for me. I never asked her to do that. I never told her I needed her. I just showed up in her life on November 22, 1956, and I never left. Mom wasn't perfect. She made mistakes, but she was always doing her best to care for me. Even when I didn't like what she was doing, she still did what she thought was best for me. Even when I got angry, she still did things the way she thought was best for me.

Now, I had to do my best for her. Even when she got angry. Even when she didn't understand, and even though she never asked me.

She knew.

I know.

And my dad will know. One time when Mom was angry at me, I looked at her and said, "Mom, I'm only doing what Dad told me to do. He gave me specific instructions about how I was to handle things. I'm doing exactly what he said to do."

Then, I leaned forward and held her hands, "Mom, you're looking at the only man who'll need two votes to get into heaven. When I get up there, Jesus will say, 'Well done, good and faithful servant.' Then, Dad will step around the throne and say to Jesus, 'Hold on,

Jesus, I've got a few questions I need to ask the boy. Mike, son, did you take care of your mother the way I told you to?'"

"Yes sir, I did."

When you're dealing with an Alzheimer's patient, there are many days when you aren't sure you're doing the right thing. You can do it this way or that way, and no one seems to know which way would be best. You're just doing the best you know how.

And in the end, that's all you can do—the best you can. If you can look in the mirror and know you did the best you could do given the information you had, you'll be able to live with that. And that's important because you'll be living with yourself for a really long time.

Coffee with Mom:
"One day, I'm going to see your dad, and I'm going to tell him what a lousy job you've done taking care of me."

Chapter 18

Until I Can't Say Goodbye Anymore

One of the hard things about having to deal with an Alzheimer's patient is having to listen to all of the well-meaning advice and counsel from everyone you meet who has someone with Alzheimer's in their family.

And everyone has someone in their family suffering from the illness. They may have just died, almost died, or died a long time ago, but the details don't seem to matter. For some reason, people feel like they need to tell you everything they've been through on their journey. Most of the time it doesn't help. For one thing, the illness affects everyone differently. Some people get angry. Some become violent. Some become quiet and withdrawn while others become childlike. People

> **Coffee with Mom:**
> "You're not preaching my funeral. No way I'm giving you the last word."

166

mean well. I know they do, but a lot of times someone else's pain just adds to your own.

But there was one friend, Dr. Robert Bishop, who shared something with me that I never forgot. He had lost his mother to Alzheimer's a few years before. Unlike my mother, his mother got to the point where she didn't know him at all. Toward the end, she didn't respond to him either.

"But I wouldn't trade a minute of it," he told me. "I wouldn't give back one minute when I got to sit with her and hold her hand and tell her I loved her. No, I'd keep every minute. So, my advice to you," he said, "is to hold on to every moment. The time will come when you won't have any moments. Don't waste one of them."

For some reason, that counsel stayed with me. Whenever I really didn't feel like going to see Mom, I would remember Robert's words, and I would stop by. Sometimes I would wonder if I was doing any good at all, and again I'd remember his words.

One of the things I discovered is you have to find your own reasons to care for your aging parent. I really couldn't expect anything from Mom. If I thought she was going to be grateful for the care I was giving her or if she was going to participate with me in her care, I was sadly mistaken. For one thing, she wasn't able to do that, and second, if my mom had been capable, I would have had another battle on my hands altogether.

I would go and see her. Sometimes, she'd be hostile. Other times, she would be silent in her anger. Sometimes she'd be funny, and other days she would almost be her old self. We'd tell stories and laugh, and she'd want to know about the grandchildren and the church. And I soaked up every moment.

I learned not to fight with her. Trying to argue with her was a waste of time. For one thing, she couldn't keep her mind focused long enough to have a real argument. Something I would say would distract her, or she would just wander off to a new target. I found myself so frustrated because we could never finish an argument. Then, I realized that was my fault. I was expecting my mom to do something she could not do.

I learned to just roll with wherever she was. If she wanted to talk about buying a car, I'd talk about buying her a car. I knew I was never going to buy her a car, but that never stopped her from talking to me about her getting a car.

"Have you bought me a car yet?"

"No, ma'am, I haven't."

"Have you even looked?"

"Yes, I have."

"I want my Suburban back."

"Mom, that's a big car. Don't you want something a little smaller?"

"No, I want my Suburban. Don't you remember how I would throw the boys in the back of that car and off we'd go to the lake house?"

"Yes, ma'am, I remember. I miss the lake house."

"I do too," Mom would say. Then, we'd talk about the lake house. "Your daddy loved that lake house." Then, we'd talk about Dad.

Toward the end, I was having to bring all of the energy to the conversation. Mom would remember, or at least become animated in a manner suggesting she had remembered, and she would laugh at our favorite family stories.

I would show her pictures of my granddaughters and she would "ooh" and "ahh" over them like it was the first time she had seen them. It was. She couldn't remember we had looked at the same pictures the day before.

I wasn't getting anything back from her. She would absorb all of the energy I would bring to the conversation. Some days, I would be exhausted as I finally got into my office around nine in the morning. I had been carrying Mom throughout our entire conversation and this, of course, would bring back all of my grief. While it's true that you lose them a little bit at a time, some days you lose more of them than others.

I cried every day. Some days, I wouldn't cry that much, but I would still cry. Walking back to my car or driving to the church or just sitting in my desk chair and feeling the weight settle down on me. The weight of grieving for all that had been lost. The struggle of having to see my mom so helpless. She would have been horrified if she could have seen herself. I hurt for her. I missed my dad. I missed her.

And I didn't know how much longer we would have to keep walking down this road. But then, I would remember Robert's words . . . and I'd go see her the next day. And I would keep dropping by to see her until I couldn't go see her anymore.

We ran out of time on Saturday morning, July 14, 2018. I had been out of town, and my flight had been canceled and rerouted. I ended up getting home twelve hours later than I should have. Jeannie had gone to lunch with Mom and told me they had a pretty good time. I was planning to go see her the next morning.

Coffee with Mom:
"One cup of coffee
doesn't count
as a visit."

The phone rang at six o'clock.

"Don't come to Morning Pointe," the nurse's voice said. "Go to Williamson Medical Center. Your mom has had some kind of episode, and we're sending her to the emergency room." Jeannie and I both got up and started to get dressed. She called Morning Pointe and confirmed the details of Mom's condition. We didn't know much; but we did know Mom had lost consciousness, and it didn't look good.

We were at the hospital a few minutes later, and we beat the ambulance to the hospital. A very understanding hospital staff showed me where to park the car and where to stand to wait on the ambulance. I know it was only a few minutes, but we waited for what seemed like hours. Finally, the ambulance backed up to the hospital doors and the emergency medical techs rolled Mom into the emergency room. Mom was DNR (Do Not Resuscitate), but the techs hadn't gotten that word. They had tried their best to keep Mom alive. They shocked her three times and were performing CPR as they brought her in.

I told them she was DNR, and they stopped and tried to explain it wasn't their fault, but that really wasn't my concern and my mom had already been hurt enough.

The doctor got her stable, but it was apparent that Mom wasn't going to recover. Her oxygen saturation rate was 80 and dropping. Her blood pressure was failing. The doctor told us he would give us a minute, which is doctor speak for "I think she's about to die." So, he stepped out and left me in the room with my mom, my wife, and my mom's three sisters. We sat quietly and watched Mom.

Then, to everyone's surprise, Mom began to recover. While she never regained consciousness, her blood pressure stabilized, and her breathing improved. With her numbers improving, the doctor stepped in to suggest we plan to admit her, and we agreed.

When the doctor left, my aunt leaned next to me and said, "Michael, I believe Jesus is having second thoughts." The picture of Jesus reaching for the heavenly gates and then hesitating as He thought about letting Mom in cracked us all up. I don't know what people would have thought if they had looked into the room and saw my mom in the bed and all of us standing around laughing until we cried.

We did admit her, but it didn't matter. It was only a matter of time. We sat there and watched her breathe. We said what we needed to say.

And then, she just stopped breathing. There was nothing dramatic. No last words. She exhaled, and then, she never inhaled again.

We gathered up her things, and we went home. We had her funeral service at Brentwood Baptist Church, and from the crowd, you would have thought a local dignitary had passed away. My mom told me she had more friends in the church than I did. From the number in attendance, I'm not sure she was wrong.

Her favorite musicians played and sang. Chris and Craig, my sons and her grandsons, both spoke. Craig told the story of Mom carrying a wooden spoon to discipline them when they were little. One Sunday, when they were little, he asked "Bob Bob" (the name her grandchildren called her) if she had the spoon. She nodded her head that she did. Feeling bold, he said he wanted to see it.

Without ever looking at Craig, she slid her hand into her purse and pulled the spoon out so Craig could see it. According to Craig, the mere sight of the spoon inspired good behavior.

The graveside was a large affair. She was buried next to my dad, and her friends, many from as long as fifty years ago, gathered around and began to tell stories. The places they had shopped, the places they had travelled, and the adventures they shared. I thought I knew my mother pretty well, but I was hearing stories I had never heard before. My parents had been quite the celebrities. Everyone wanted to be their friend. Everyone wanted them to be at the party. "They just don't make them like her anymore," I was told more than once.

I know that now in a way I never have. Like I said, when you're little, you think everyone has a mom like you. I was surprised to realize they don't. Then, you realize *no one* has a mother like you do. She's one of a kind.

And I was privileged to be her son. I was honored to be the one who cared for her. I was the one she counted on, and I wouldn't trade that for anything.

Shortly after Mom passed away, Regie Ragland pulled me aside at church one Sunday morning. Regie is the community director at Morning Pointe and became a good friend to my mom and an invaluable resource to me.

"I've been wanting to tell you this story. On Friday, before your mother died, we had our worship service. Since your mom loved the music, I went and got her to come with me to the service. After we sang, I got up to serve communion, and your mother got up with me. She stood next to me, and I thought, *Well, that would be okay,* and I let her stand there. Then, as our friends came to receive communion, your mom helped me serve communion. She talked with each person and prayed with most of them. That's the last picture I have of your mom. It was a beautiful moment I'll never forget."

My mom serving communion . . . she was in a place she didn't want to be. She couldn't do the things she wanted to do or live the life that she wanted to live, but there she was. Praying with the residents and sharing the bread and cup.

> **Coffee with Mom:**
> Today was the first day I drove to the church without stopping to have coffee with Mom. Grief has a quiet way of sneaking up on you when you start thinking you're "over it."

That was my mom. Life may be tough, but it's never too tough that you can't gather around a table, share a little bread, and remind someone how much they are loved.

That's what my mom did.

And I'll never drink another cup of coffee and not think about her.

Chapter 19

Things No One Will Tell You (But You Need to Hear Anyway)

If you're like me, you play a lot of "what if" in your head. As much as I can, I try to anticipate what will happen and think through my response to them. Sometimes, I think through conversations and try to think about how to respond when I'm in a meeting with this person or that committee. I think through what I'll do if this happens or that happens. More than once in my life, I've been able to be prepared for a variety of situations because, believe it

Coffee with Mom:
In the end, you have to live with yourself. If you can remember, in all of the craziness of the disease, the only thing that really matters is knowing you did the best you could, you'll be fine. Less than that is hard to live with.

or not, I had already thought through what I would do if this or that did happen. When it did, I was ready.

I never thought through what I would do if Mom was diagnosed with Alzheimer's and vascular dementia. My father would never live long enough to face this illness. His heart wouldn't let him. We'd known for a long time my dad would die of heart disease. One of his doctors told me he was surprised every time he came into his office and was not told my dad had died the night before. I had thought through this scenario. I knew what I would do when I got the phone call to get to Huntsville as fast as I could.

But not with Mom. How could I have seen it? Her grandmother lived well into her nineties. Her father was in his eighties when he died—and he was a serious smoker for most of his life. None of her relatives had dealt with this. Her sisters were all healthy. My mom would die, one day, but only after a long and adventurous life.

Do you want to know what scenario I had been thinking about? I was worried Mom was going to live so long she was going to outlive her resources. She and Dad had done well, but there are limits to everything. What would Jeannie and I do if she lived one year, five years, ten years past what she could pay for? What was I going to do if she lived to be ninety? Or one hundred? Mom would tell me she was going to live as long as she could just to annoy me.

I wasn't ready when the illness came. I wasn't ready when she died. For four years, I faced day after day not being ready for what I had to face. What could I have done to get ready? What do I wish I had known? What do I wish someone had told me?

I wish I had known that on most days, there are no right or wrong answers. There's only the best you can do. I spent hours and hours and too many sleepless nights trying to figure out what was the best thing to do when there was no "best" way to do it. What if Mom lives here? What if she lives there? In the end, it really didn't matter.

I wish someone had told me to act as soon as I saw the first evidence of a problem. Yes, it would have been hard. My mom would have fought me every step of the way, but she fought me anyway. At least if I had acted earlier, I would have had the chance of dealing with my mom while she was still somewhat rational. As it was, I had to make these hard decisions, fight with my mom, and also try to cope with the irrationality of her disease. I'm a natural procrastinator, but I wished someone had told me that actions put off only get more and more difficult by the moment.

But it is hard to act. The first time you see something off, something out of place, your patient will always have a perfectly logical explanation for why things are the way they are. If a bill is left unpaid, it's only because she's been so overwhelmed by her grief.

If there's a scratch on the car, it's the teenagers in the neighborhood.

But I knew better. I just couldn't allow myself to say it. If I spoke the words, everything would change. To be honest, I panicked. I wish someone had told me about that moment when you look at your mom and realize something is wrong and your blood goes cold. You shiver because you're freezing inside. You tremble, because now, you're the adult. Now, you're going to be making the decisions. One moment, your mom makes all the decisions. Then, you're offering your input to her decisions, and next, you're making all the decisions and having to totally disregard your mother's input—something I had never done in my life—because her input is totally incoherent.

And I mean ALL the decisions. Where she will live, what she will wear, what doctors will treat her, and what treatment she'll have. There are just some decisions a son shouldn't have to make for his mother, but you have to make them and make them you will. You do what love requires, and if love requires you to talk to your mom about her problem with incontinence, well, that's what you do.

No one can prepare you when you become the adult and your parent becomes the child.

And you have to do something. I wish someone had told me this earlier . . . and louder. **There comes a moment when you have to act.** I did act, but I acted much too late. I should have acted and acted decisively much sooner than I did. For one thing, your patient isn't going to act. They can't. As far as they know, life is great. There's nothing wrong at all.

And it's not going to get any better. This day is the best day you'll have.

I wish someone could have told me that some days are harder than others, but the hard days aren't the days you expect. Going to doctors' appointments and expecting bad news—you learn to handle these moments because you expect them. You brace yourself for them.

The hard moments are when your mom looks like your mom, but then says or does something that reminds you she's not your mom anymore. You sit next to her and, for the moment, everything looks like it's supposed to. You allow yourself to relax and think everything is okay. You're okay. She's okay, and the two of you are drinking coffee just like you did all of your lives. Then, she'll say something that will make absolutely no sense and it will hit you. All of your grief will hit you in that moment, and you'll feel like you've been caught by a wave at the beach—one of the waves that sneaks up behind you and throws you against the ocean bottom, turning you over and over and not letting you up.

Those are bad days. **I wish someone had told me there are going to be bad days. Really bad days.** You need to have a little space in your calendar to grieve. Not allowing your grief to be expressed means the grief will find another way to be expressed. You'll find yourself exhausted, unable to sleep, suffering headaches and all kinds of other ailments because your soul is trying to tell you how badly you're hurting. You have to pay attention to this.

I loved people who would walk up and give me a quick hug and just say, "Praying for you and your mom." They wouldn't stay long enough for me to say anything back. They wouldn't ask. They would just love me in the moment and move on. I loved this because, first, I was glad to know someone was thinking about us, and second, there were days when I couldn't answer. Well, I couldn't have answered without tearing up. Some days, the emotion would be just under my skin. I was afraid if I was jostled at all, I would dissolve into a puddle of little-boy tears.

Coffee with Mom:
Savor every moment, even the difficult ones. Moments, sooner or later, all run out.

I loved people who loved my mom. As I write this, I have been the pastor of Brentwood Baptist Church for more than twenty-seven years. I love this church, and I love them more for the way they loved my mom. The Nurture Team, the women's pastoral care ministry of our church, pulled my mother in like she was an honored guest. They welcomed her until the day my mother couldn't physically or mentally be part of their ministry. On bad days when she couldn't grasp what they were trying to do, they insisted she play the old hymns for them on a nearby piano. On good days, she worked as hard as they did. She always came away from that moment with stories and laughter. The women let her know she was loved and valued. For many parents the rule is simple: if you love my child, I'll love you. For children caring for their aging parents, the rule is just as simple, only reversed: **Love my mother, and I'll love you.**

There were several families and individuals who became close to my mom. They would drop by and pick her up to ride off on some grand adventure. She would send me pictures taken at a local museum, standing next to an Elvis statue or sitting in some local barbecue joint listening to bluegrass music. I love these pictures. For just a moment, I had a snapshot of my mom. The mom I used to know. The mom who loved an adventure and seeing new things. She would fade away into the shadows of her illness fast enough, but for that moment, I would have her back.

I loved talking to her old friends and her family, especially her sisters. **I loved hearing the old stories about who my mom used to be.** I wanted all of the stories I could hear. Mom was forgetting them, and I was afraid I would too. So, when someone said, "Did your mom ever tell you about . . . ?" I would say, "no," even if she had. I wanted to hear it again. I wanted to be sure I hadn't forgotten any detail. I wanted to be sure the story I heard was the story I remembered. When you're on this journey, memory can play some funny tricks on you.

I loved friends who would just listen. Sometimes, you just don't know what to do next. You need a safe place to lay out all of your options and just work through them one at a time. Some of your ideas won't work, but some of them will. You'll need a little time to work through them. You'll begin to see what's viable and what's not pretty quickly, but the last thing you need is someone pointing out all the holes of your thinking. Most of the time, my feelings were so raw, when someone would point out an error, I would get angry. I felt like I was being picked on, like my friends were piling on. Good friends would just listen and then ask, "So, what do you think you're going to do?"

I was always glad to hear that people were praying for me, but those who took the time to write a card were especially meaningful. You can hold onto a card. You can pull it out and read it again. If the card is funny, you can laugh again. If the card is meaningful, you can meditate on what it meant to you when you read it and then, when you reread it, the meaning will come back to you, or the meaning will be enhanced as the meaning has changed mainly because you have changed.

I finally started keeping a journal. I've kept a journal for years, but I needed a "Mom Journal." I needed to keep a detailed record of conversations, observations, and thoughts. I wish I had taken pictures. I wish I had taken pictures of what the house looked like, the small dents and scratches in her car. I wish I had written down every conversation with Mom as soon as they happened. By the time I "found the time," we'd been through six or seven other conversations. I couldn't keep track of everything.

Those tiny moments of self-doubt and confusion were the only thing Mom needed to throw me off the plan or make me look like I was either inept or evil. I wish I had a way, in those moments, to be able to pull out something she couldn't argue with—like a receipt or a picture. I think that would have helped.

Or, maybe it wouldn't have. She was one who would never let reality change her mind.

Most of all, I appreciated those friends who knew even though I was sixty-one years old at the time, I was still a nine-year-old little boy inside. There's something about your mother. It's doesn't matter how old she is or how old you are. You're just nine years old inside. You're just a little boy who wants his mom to get better, and now knows she never will be.

She's gone. Now, you're the adult. I wish someone had told me it's really not any fun being an adult.

Coffee with Mom:
Nobody loves her son like a mother. I miss being loved like that. I was always smart, handsome, and strong—and Mom never let me forget it.

Chapter 20

Loving Your Parents When You Really Don't Like Them

I've always been frustrated by the apostle Paul's instructions to fathers in Ephesians 6. "Fathers," he writes, "don't stir up anger in your children" (Eph. 6:4). Some versions translate the verse, "don't frustrate your children." Paul seems to be telling fathers, "Listen, your kids will be okay as long as you don't mess them up."

> **Coffee with Mom:**
> "I've noticed since I've been here, you haven't preached on honoring your parents."

Really, isn't that disappointing? Don't we expect something more from Paul? Shouldn't his teaching to fathers be, well, more inspirational? Wouldn't we want Paul to say, "Raise up children who are strong in their faith"? Or, "Raise up those who will follow Christ bravely"? We don't get any of that. All Paul says is, "Dads, don't mess the kids up."

I really didn't understand this verse until I started teaching at a Tuesday night worship event for young adults at our church called Kairos. Most of these young adults were still in college or just graduating and beginning their careers. The more I got to know them, the more stories I heard, and the more stories I heard, the more this verse made sense.

A lot of these young adults had difficult relationships with their fathers. Some of them had no relationship at all with their dads. Because of this, they had a hard time understanding the person of God. Anytime I mentioned God loved them like a father, a lot of them would look down. They had been abandoned by their fathers, betrayed by their fathers, even abused by their fathers. Having God love them like that isn't something they wanted.

Finally, I began to understand what Paul was talking about. He was simply saying:

"Fathers, don't make it hard to believe in God."

The most fundamental understanding we have of God is God as Father. If you have a good dad, as I did, then believing God loves you is an easy step to make. When I was little, I announced to my parents, "God had buttons." What I meant by that was God sat in front of a very large computer, and if He wanted it to rain in Tennessee, He'd press a few buttons, the weather would come up on His screen, and it would rain in Tennessee.

I know. That's a rather simple understanding of God, but it made sense to me. Why? Because my father worked on the radar system of the Hawk missile. He had taken me to work and shown me the large radar scopes with flashing green lights on the system. In my little mind, I figured God would have a computer screen like my dad, only it would be a whole lot bigger. For a child, this wasn't a bad way of thinking.

But what happens when you don't have a good father? What happens when you don't have a good mother?

And then, what happens when they get sick? What happens when they need you?

When some of my friends found out I was writing this book, they would tell me, "You're lucky. You had a great mom and dad. It's not that way for me."

Another friend sent me a text, "Are you going to say anything in your book about what happens when the dad you haven't seen in twenty years suddenly wants back into your life? I don't know if I want him back in my life. Is that wrong?"

The hard choices in life aren't between good and bad. We do pretty well with those. The hard choices in life are between good and best, bad and worse. Sometimes we fail when we could have chosen best but only choose good, and other times, we can only choose bad and thank God it's not any worse. Sometimes life doesn't give you good choices . . . or easy ones either.

First, let me be forcefully blunt. There are some people who are dangerous. They have done evil in the past, and we have no indication they won't do evil again. I wish it wasn't this way, but we live in a very broken world. There are fathers who have abused their daughters. There are mothers who have abused their sons. There are homes filled with violence and addictions whose stories would make Stephen King blush. I know. I've seen these families. The children didn't just leave these homes; they escaped.

Please hear me. At no time does Jesus expect you to put yourself or your family in danger. Paul reminds us to live in peace with people "as far as it depends on you" (Rom. 12:18). Sometimes, it's not up to us. Humpty Dumpty couldn't be put back together. There are some relationships and some families that can't be repaired unless God strikes the home with a bolt of lightning. You shouldn't feel guilty. You shouldn't beat yourself up for not having a relationship with your parents.

There's a reason Jesus gave us permission to dust off our sandals and walk away. There are situations like this across America. Fathers have been so bad, mothers have been so bad, they forfeit any right to be part of their children's lives. I know that's harsh, but that's reality. Yes, I believe Christ can change people's lives, but each person has to give Christ permission to work. Without this permission, Christ won't do any mighty works. Just as He left His hometown without doing anything because of their unbelief, Jesus will walk away from anyone who won't open the door for Him.

I know these situations are rare, but they are the only reality some of our friends know. That's why inter-generational groups are so important in church life. This is the place where the Father recreates the family unit. Those without a father, find a father. Those without a mother, find a mother, and those without children find scores of them—and grandchildren too!

Relationships with our parents are foundational relationships of human life. We are formed and shaped by our mothers and fathers, for better or for worse. This is why this relationship is addressed right in the middle of the Ten Commandments. As the Israelites moved into the Promised Land, God gave His people ten laws that would define their relationships with Him and each other. The fifth commandment says, "Honor your father and your mother so that you may have a long life in the land that the LORD your God is giving you" (Exod. 20:12).

As others have noticed, this is the first command-ment with a promise attached, but notice something else. The commandment is directed to the children, not the parents. I would have thought the commandment would be directed to the parents, something like, "Raise up good kid," or, "Take your children to church."

It's not. It's directed to the children who are com-manded to "honor" their parents. The parents don't even have to be worth honoring—there's no descriptive clause here—for the children to be required to honor them. This verse is never qualified or watered down. It says what it means, and it means what it says.

What it says is there is something about people who love God that is shown by the way they honor their parents. As in many other aspects of our lives, our actions are never dictated by others, but only by our obedience to Christ.

So, what does that mean? How do you honor a parent who isn't worthy of the honor?

First, we're grateful to them for giving us life. The circumstances of our birth may not have been idyllic, and our home life may never have been a Norman Rockwell painting, but for better or worse, you're here, and you're here because of them.

If for nothing else, we're grateful to them and honor them for bringing us into the world.

Second, we forgive them. Most of the time, our mothers and fathers were doing the best they could. If they failed, they didn't intend to fail. They made bad decisions without ever understanding the consequences of their decisions. Other times, mothers and fathers were mean and evil. Either way, forgiveness is something we offer to them, not something they ask for from us.

Forgiveness, simply put, is releasing the other person from the expectation they can fix what they did. If your parents hurt you, they could apologize a thousand times, and it wouldn't heal the pain in your life. Only Christ can bring that kind of healing. No one else can do it. When we stop waiting for other people to "fix" what they've done, we are free to find another way to move on.

Third, if we can't help, we don't hurt. Again, our behavior is always in response to the grace of Christ in our life. Just because your mother or father hurt you doesn't give you the right to hurt them. If it's best for you not to have a relationship with your parents, fine, but don't go out of your way to "make them pay" or "give them what they deserve." Judging others isn't in our job description. We don't help anyone, including ourselves, when we only try to make things worse.

Next, ask yourself, what would you do for a stranger? If you didn't know your mother or father at all, but they were simply someone who was going through a hard time, what would you do? Would you call them? Would you send a card? Would you visit? How would you act if you had no relationship with them at all?

In reality, this is where you are. The old is gone, buried with Christ. The new is possible in the resurrection of Jesus. You're not going to rebuild the old relationship. That's over. If there is to be a relationship at all, it will be something new Jesus does in the power of His resurrection. The greatest journeys all start with one step. Don't be afraid to take small steps in this new relationship. Rome wasn't built in a day, and it wasn't torn down in a day either. It won't be rebuilt in a day either. Mercy takes its own time.

How would you act if your parent was a friend? Would you cook them a meal? Watch a ball game with them? Let's face it. For some of us, being friends with our parents would be a victory worth celebrating. So, if you can't be mother and child or father and child, can you at least be friends?

Let's go back to the heart of this commandment. This is about you, not your parents. This is about the type of person you are and what you believe about redemption, grace, forgiveness, mercy, and love. This is where our theology of Easter is tested. Yes, I did say there are relationships beyond repair, but I also said these were rare. Truth is, there are very few relationships that can't be mended or even made better. But it starts with you. What kind of relationship do you want? What do you need from your mother or father? What are you hoping they will bring to your life? It's important to understand your expectations. Some expectations are unrealistic and can't be met. Others are vital to what you're seeking. Do you know what your expectations are? Can you share them? Knowing them might be a good place to start the conversation.

You're free to take whatever steps you feel the need to take or led to take by the Spirit. We are not trapped by guilt or manipulated by neurotic needs. We are free in Christ to release old wounds and relationships. We are free in Christ to build new ones. We're also free in Christ to let it go and never remember it again. In Christ, we have choices.

Just don't expect to be perfect. Nothing in our world ever is. Sometimes, close enough or good enough is all we can expect. Don't let your expectations be defined by others. All of your well-meaning church buddies will tell you to "trust God" or "just pray about it." It's good advice; it just doesn't help very much in real life. Every situation is different, and there is no "one size fits all" response.

> **Coffee with Mom:**
> Your parents' anger at you is a left-handed compliment. They feel free to be angry at you because they know you won't leave them. It doesn't feel like a statement of trust, but it really is.

This is your journey. This is how Christ is working in your life to fashion you more into His likeness. Trust Him. Trust His ways. That will be enough. That will always be enough.

Chapter 21

The Best of "Coffee with Mom" Tweets

"Are you taking care of my Christmas shopping? You're not getting anything for you, are you?"

"Bring me some of my Alabama stuff. Everybody around here is wearing Tennessee orange." (Gotta love my mom!)

"I'm glad you came by today. I'm very busy this week, and I don't have time to sit around and wait on you."

"This biscuit is colder than a frog's fanny. How do you expect me to eat a biscuit that won't melt butter?"

193

"Well, if you're not going to buy me a car, get me a chauffeur like that lady in the movie."

"I heard you had the flu . . . I was praying for something worse."

"You're running a little late this morning, but you're a Baptist preacher. You don't know anything about time."

"I wish I had something exciting to tell you, but we just sat around and looked at each other today."

"I had a visitor yesterday. You know her . . . you know . . . oh, why can't you think of her name?"

"Can you come back later? I'm playing the piano now."

"My friends tell me you've been talking about me. How do you get on that Internet thing so I can talk about you?"

"You don't understand, son. Without your dad, there is no 'us.' It's just 'me.' I miss 'us.'"

"I think I may try another church. I just know too much on this preacher." (Meaning me, of course.)

When I told her I was tweeting her comments: "Well, now, everyone knows where you got your smarts from."

"Your sermon was short. [I went about 22 minutes.] After all week, I thought you would've come up with a little more."

Acknowledgments

No book is ever written by itself, and this one certainly wasn't. There were countless people, too many to name, who were part of this journey. There were some, however, that Mom would have wanted me to be sure to mention.

I'm grateful for Dr. Paul Newhouse, whose care and treatment of my mother gave us a deep sense of peace that we were doing all we could do. His gentle way with Mom will not be forgotten.

Dr. George L. Holmes was her family physician and joined Mom's care when she was already advanced in her illness. Still, Lanny knew what to say and what to do—both for my mom and for me.

The good people at Morning Pointe in Brentwood loved my mom well, especially Regie Ragland, Chris Phillips, and Lori Simpson.

The congregation of Brentwood Baptist Church gave me the space I needed to care for my mom and treated my mom like visiting royalty.

The Nurture Team of Brentwood Baptist Church welcomed my mom into their ministry and gave her meaning and purpose. Their love for her won't be forgotten.

I'm grateful for her sisters, Dianne, Karleen, and Jenny, who supported my decisions and encouraged me along the way.

A special word of thanks to Beverly Clecker, Lorraine Quist, and Kim Cox. Mom loved going on adventures with you.

To my wife, Jeannie . . . I couldn't have done this without you. Your strength and wisdom got me through more than one day.

To Jaclyn Swencki, my executive assistant—how you kept all of this in order I'll never know.

And to Devin Maddox, who thought a book like this may be helpful to some who are on this journey. I pray he's right.